TWAYNE'S WORLD AUTHORS SERIES

A Survey of the World's Literature

GREECE

John P. Anton, Emory University

EDITOR

Aristophanes

TWAS 482

ARISTOPHANES

By LOIS SPATZ

University of Missouri-Kansas City

TWAYNE PUBLISHERS

A DIVISION OF G. K. HALL & CO., BOSTON

Library of Congress Cataloging in Publication Data

Spatz, Lois.
  Aristophanes.

  (Twayne's world authors series ; TWAS 482 : Greece)
  Bibliography: p. 161 - 64
  Includes index.
  1.   Aristophanes—Criticism and interpretation.
PA3879.S67   882'.01   77-27620
ISBN 0-8057-6323-6

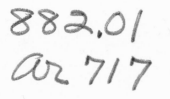
To Jonas
animae dimidio meae

Contents

About the Author

Dr. Lois Settler Spatz graduated from Goucher College in 1960 as a Phi Beta Kappa with Honors in Classics. She received her Ph.D. in Classics from Indiana University in 1968. After teaching at Brooklyn College and Park College, she is now a member of the English Department at the University of Missouri-Kansas City. Although Dr. Spatz teaches Greek or Latin whenever possible, she specializes in courses in drama, mythology, and ancient literature in translation. She has reviewed several books on these subjects for *Classical Journal* and *American Classical Review*. She chose *Strophic Construction in Aristophanic Lyric* as her dissertation topic and has pursued that interest by publishing "Metrical Motivs in Aristophanes' *Clouds*," *Quaderni Urbinati*, 13 (1972) pp. 62 - 82 and now the present volume on Aristophanes. Dr. Spatz is currently preparing a book on Aeschylus for the Twayne Greek Author Series.

Preface

This book is addressed to the reader who has laughed at Aristophanes' wit and unrestrained obscenity without realizing that his humor had an important place in the community life of fifth-century Athens. Therefore, I have emphasized the historical context and social function of his genre, Old Comedy.

The first chapter explains the connection between comedy and the widespread worship of the nature deity, Dionysus. Comedy provided the worshippers of Dionysus with ceremonial or sacred release from anxiety about death and the unknown. Particular aspects of the sacred release are studied in the chapters where they are most relevant. For example, the functions of obscenity and sexual humor are explored in the context of *Archarnians* and *Lysistrata*, while the ubiquitous satire of the gods receives special treatment in *Birds*.

The sacred release also helped the spectator to come to terms with the problems and restraints, both private and public, of his own daily life. In Aristophanes' typical comic fantasy, the hero, representing the average Athenian, is a crafty underdog who conceives of an ingenious scheme by which he frees himself from various types of oppression. Because Aristophanes derived his material from real life, I have presented each play in its historical and social context, discussing not only its particular satiric targets, but also its function in satisfying the psychological needs of the audience.

The needs of the audience were satisfied by the form as well as the content of Old Comedy. The form is unique, containing a chorus which sings elaborate lyrics, a limited number of actors who speak the argot of the streets, and a dramatic structure which defies the canons of logical order. The first chapter discusses the art form itself, with all its peculiarities, and explains the details of its origin and production, so far as they are known. Subsequent chapters are concerned with the poet's dramatic and literary devices (such as the juxtaposition of fantasy and reality, the order of episodes, and the imagery) and their relation to the theme of the play and the functions of Old Comedy.

The plays have been discussed in the order of production. The treatment of each major play begins with a description of the situation in Athens and a brief summary of the plot. The detailed analysis which follows examines the objects and dramatic devices of the satire. The concluding section is concerned with such topics as the significance of the social criticism and the nature of the sacred release.

Because the corpus of Aristophanes' extant plays is so large, I have found it necessary to limit my treatment of his less famous works. Three minor plays have been connected to the major ones to which they are most closely related in theme. Thus, a short section on *Peace* follows the detailed analysis of *Acharnians*, the first play on the question of ending the Peloponnesian War. A brief discussion of *Knights*, which ridicules a current demagogue, precedes the full treatment of the later play *Birds*, a satire of the entire democracy. Aristophanes' last two plays, *Ekklēsiazousai (Women in the Assembly)* and *Wealth*, so different from his earlier, more exuberant Old Comedies, have been discussed together. The lost works or plays that survive only in fragments have not been mentioned unless they are relevant to the subject under discussion. The annotated bibliography, however, lists both the primary and secondary sources pertinent to the remains of Old Comedy.

I have stressed the artistic and social aspects of Aristophanes' works at the expense of the more technical problems that concern classical scholars. I have accepted as standard the text edited by Victor Coulon and translated by H. Van Daele (Paris: Budé, 1954 - 1964) without discussing complex questions such as variant readings, number of speaking roles, and change of speaker. Aspects of diction and meter and the intricacies of parody have been presented in general terms only, while disputes concerning the dating or facts of production are mentioned only briefly in the text or relegated to the notes. Nor have I been able to provide complete information about the daily life in Athens that forms the background for the comedies. I have indicated, however, where evidence is scant and conclusions tentative, and I have referred in the notes and bibliography to fuller discussions of ideas introduced in the text. The labors of classical scholars in all these areas have made my own analysis possible, and I hope that my references will encourage both Greek and Greekless readers to study the subject further.

Preface

Three critical studies have been particularly helpful for the analysis of the social functions and artistic devices of Old Comedy:

K. J. Dover, *Aristophanic Comedy* (Berkeley and Los Angeles: University of California Press, 1972).

Hermann Weber, "Aristophanes and his Sense of the Comic: A Comparative Study of the Meaning of Old Comedy" (Ph.D. diss., University of Texas at Austin, 1968).

Cedric Whitman, *Aristophanes and the Comic Hero* (Cambridge, Mass.: Harvard University Press, 1964).

I would like to thank the typing pool, headed by Mrs. Alice Smith, in the Office of the Dean of the College of Arts and Sciences at the University of Missouri-Kansas City. I would also like to acknowledge the editor of this series, Professor John P. Anton of Emory University, for his careful reading and constructive advice about the manuscript. I am particularly grateful to my sons, Stephen and David, who patiently endured the demands of this sibling, and to my husband, Jonas, who bestowed all the love, understanding, and concrete help of an expectant father in bringing this book to birth.

Lois Spatz

University of Missouri-Kansas City

Chronology

450 B.C.?   Birth of Aristophanes.

431 B.C.   Beginning of the Peloponnesian War between Athens and Sparta.

429 B.C.   Death of Pericles.

427 B.C.   Sophists Gorgias and Tisias visit Athens. *Daitalēs (Banqueters;* not extant)

426 B.C.   *Babylōnioi (Babylonians;* not extant). Possible indictment of Aristophanes for lese majesty.

425 B.C.   *Akharnēs (Acharnians).*

424 B.C.   *Hippēs (Knights).*

423 B.C.   *Nephelai (Clouds;* original version lost; extant play is later revision).

422 B.C.   *Sphēkes (Wasps).*

421 B.C.   *Eirēnē (Peace).* Peace of Nicias between Athens and Sparta.

415 B.C.   Athenian Expedition to Sicily.

414 B.C.   *Ornithes (Birds).*

413 B.C.   *Lysistratē (Lysistrata); Thesmophoriazousai.* Oligarchic revolution at Athens. Restoration of democracy.

406 B.C.   Death of Sophocles and Euripides. Battle of Arginusae.

405 B.C.   *Batrakhoi (Frogs).* Battle of Aegospotami.

404 B.C.   Surrender of Athens. Year of the Thirty Tyrants.

403 B.C.   Restoration of democracy after civil war.

399 B.C.   Death of Socrates.

395 B.C.   Revival of Athenian power. New alliances and resumption of hostilities against Sparta.

392 B.C.?   *Ekklēsiazousai (Women in the Assembly).*

388 B.C.   *Ploutos (Wealth).*

385 B.C.?   Death of Aristophanes. Posthumous productions of *Aiolosikōn* and *Kōkalos* (neither extant).

CHAPTER 1

Aristophanes' Comedy and the World of Athens

I Aristophanes' Life and Times

W E cannot hope to reconstruct the facts about the life and personality of Aristophanes from the meager details of parentage and production that have survived him. How fortunate that a younger contemporary, another maker of myth and drama, has left us his impressions of the comic genius. In Plato's dialogue *The Symposium* Aristophanes appears as a member of that group of sophisticated Athenians who gather for a celebration at the house of Agathon the poet. Greeted as a "joker and lover of jokes," the comedian, hung over from the night before, delights his companions with hiccups and sneezes as well as a fantastic tale of Love. His witty account of the androgynous origin of man reveals his knowledge of the scientific and philosophical theories of his day. He is on familiar terms with all the important people of Athens. He jests with Socrates, Alcibiades, and the tragedian Agathon as well as with a doctor and rhetorician. In Plato's judgment, Aristophanes knew his world well and recorded it accurately. When Dionysius, the tyrant of Syracuse, asked about the people and institutions of Athens, Plato is said to have sent him the comedies of Aristophanes.[1]

Little is known about the life of Aristophanes himself, but much more information is available about Athens in his lifetime.[2] From an inference based on *Clouds* (ll. 528 - 33), it is judged that he was born around 450 B.C. when Pericles was initiating the policies that gave his name to an age—the expansion of the polis (city-state) into an empire, the development of the opportunities for the lower classes to serve as officers in the democracy, and the support for an urban culture tolerant enough to nourish not only artists and thinkers but also misanthropes and quacks. In his Funeral Oration,

pronounced in honor of the dead of the first year of the Peloponnesian War, Pericles states the democratic ideal:

If we look to the laws, they afford equal justice to all in their private
differences; if to social standing, advancement in public life falls to reputation for capacity, class considerations not being allowed to interfere with
merit; nor again does poverty bar the way. . . . The freedom which we
enjoy in our government extends also to our ordinary life. There, far from
exercising a jealous surveillance over each other, we do not feel called upon
to be angry with our neighbor for doing what he likes, or even to indulge in
those injurious looks which cannot fail to be offensive . . . Further we
provide plenty of means for the mind to refresh itself from
business. . . . We throw open our city to the world, and never by alien
acts exclude foreigners from any opportunity of learning or observ-
ing . . . trusting less in system and policy than in the native spirit of our
citizens. . . .[3]

The works of Aristophanes indicate that he relished the
stimulating environment of a city that was both a local democracy
and the seat of a world empire. He took part in public life, serving
in the presidency of the council as a representative of his political
district.

Pericles delivered his Funeral Oration in 431 B.C. at the beginning of the Peloponnesian War. This power struggle with Athens'
great oligarchic rival, Sparta, lasted from 431 to 404, with only one
period of cold war, 421 to 415, when a negotiated peace was
nominally in effect. The war involved not only the two major
powers but all their allies from Sicily to the Black Sea. Victories of
one side or the other resulted in shifting populations and alliances,
and even civil wars between oligarchic and democratic factions in
city-states all over the Greek world. Eventually even the mighty
Persian empire, once beaten back by the previous generation of
Greeks, was drawn into the conflict. The war is the subject of
Thucydides' great history. It forms the background for
Aristophanes' life and works.

Eleven of the forty plays thought to have been written by him
between 427 and 388 have survived. Nine of these were produced
during the Peloponnesian War, and the fantastic plots are grounded
in the all too real vicissitudes of the battle and the political changes
that it stimulated. Three plays are directly concerned with the
problem of making peace. In *Acharnians*, the hero arranges his own
private truce with Sparta because the Athenian assembly refuses to

discuss the matter. *Peace*, produced in 421 while the Peace of Nicias was actually being negotiated, presents a hero who retrieves the long-buried Goddess of Peace for the benefit of all Greece. In *Lysistrata*, written in 411 after the renewal of hostilities and the Athenian disaster in Sicily, the women of both sides stage a sex strike to protest the war. In the fantastic world of comedy, the heroine's plan works; the warriors quickly come to terms to relieve their discomfort. But the real war was not so easily settled. Allusions to generals, policies, and Spartan power appear in all the plays. When the final defeat seemed imminent, Aristophanes actually offered his fellow citizens serious political advice in *Frogs* (405).

Although the war was the single most important historical event, it is not the only subject for Aristophanes' wit. Against the background of Athens at war, he dramatizes the major conflicts of human life itself. The hostility between the old and the young runs through all the plays and is personified in the opposition between father and son in *Clouds* and *Wasps*. Related to this theme is the conflict between those who represent "the good old days" and the reformers who have created the modern "wasteland" (*Frogs*, *Clouds*, and *Wasps*). The war between the sexes, with marriage as the battlefield, is the subject of *Thesmophoriazousai* and *Ekklesiazousai*, as well as *Lysistrata*. All the comedies pit the rich against the poor, the powerful against the oppressed. In the comic world, the underdog realizes his wildest fantasies, often by establishing a utopian society where he can satisfy his desires with impunity (*Birds*, *Ekklesiazousai*, and *Wealth*).

Aristophanes ridicules pretentiousness wherever it exists—whether in the intellectuals of *Clouds*, the poets of *Frogs* and *Thesmophoriazousai*, or the braggart soldier of *Acharnians*. Usually the affectation is exposed by the boorish comments of a fool whose simplicity appears as wisdom in contrast to the other's bombast. Indeed, the pretentiousness of society in general is mocked through constant reference to bodily functions. Although man defines himself by his reason, Aristophanes proclaims his animal nature by cramming his plays with allusions to bowels, genitals, and intercourse. Two plays are actually constructed out of dirty jokes. In *Lysistrata*, sex-starved men and women will do anything to get their partners back, while in *Thesmophoriazousai* a man impersonates a woman in order to spy on the secrets of the women's festival. The continual use of obscenity allows the audience to temporarily free themselves of the restraints of polite society and to express their ambivalent feelings about the human body. At the same time, the exposure of man's animality proclaims his ultimate union with all life and the processes of nature.

The city of Athens provides the background for this human comedy, and its institutions, attitudes, and citizens are the particulars from which the universal conflict stems. New theories of education introduced by the Sophists are distorted and ridiculed in *Clouds*, while in *Wasps* the Athenian jury system, the pride of the democracy, is exposed as fraudulent. Specific poets and poetry, so important a part of the community's culture, are constantly parodied, and, in *Thesmophoriazousai* and *Frogs*, become symbols of particular social evils. The poet harshly attacks the democratic system in *Knights* and returns to the subject of political attitudes and their effect on city life in *Birds*, where two citizens create a city in the sky as frenetic and imperialistic as the Athens they fled.

The comic poet was free to attack the most powerful individuals in the city and even to portray them in masks that exaggerated their defects.[4] Aristophanes frequently selected a well-known citizen to represent general human faults. Thus Cleon, the current demagogue, is the central figure for the attack on politicians and their dupes in *Knights*. Socrates is distorted into the Sophist par excellence in *Clouds*, whereas Euripides often appears as The Poet through whom Aristophanes mocks the high seriousness of tragedy and the failings of the younger generation (*Acharnians*, *Thesmophoriazousai*, and *Frogs*). His freedom to lampoon extended even to the gods. In *Peace* and *Birds*, Olympian deities like Hermes, Poseidon, and Zeus himself behave like gluttonous, greedy, oversexed humans. Dionysus, the hero of *Frogs*, begins as a buffoon who literally exchanges identities with his slave.

But this comedy where nothing is sacred could not survive the Peloponnesian War unchanged. In 404, the war ended disastrously for Athens. The *Frogs* of 405, produced six months before the final battle, reflects the seriousness of the situation. We have no direct information about Aristophanes in this period, but he must have lived through the government of the Thirty Tyrants put in power by Sparta, and then the civil war, when they were ejected. The indictment and death of Socrates in 399, partly for charges that the comedian himself had invented, marked the end of the age. Twenty-four years before, when the *Clouds* was produced, Socrates is reported to have stood up to show the audience how good a likeness the actor's mask was. He considered himself not slandered but teased: "When they break a jest upon me in the theater, I feel as if I were at a big party of good friends."⁵ The time for "jesting" in Athens, however, was clearly over. *Ekklēsiazousai* and *Wealth*, the two extant plays that were written after the war, contain few direct allusions to events and people. Rather they point toward a new and different kind of comedy. Aristophanes produced *Wealth* in 388, the last date we have for him. Sometime later, however, his sons, who were also dramatists, produced two other plays written by him but now lost. Thus, he must have died early in the second decade of the fourth century.

II   *The Festivals of Dionysus*

Aristophanes' comedies are intimately bound up with life in his city-state. His works were presented at a public-supported festival which the Athenians attended as part of their worship of the god Dionysus.⁶ In the month of Gamelion, roughly corresponding to January, the citizens celebrated the Lenaea which included a procession and sacrifices as well as dramatic performances in the god's sacred precinct at the base of the Acropolis. Normally five comic poets each offered one play, and, at the end of the festival, the audience judged the best three among them. Although Agathon won his first victory here in 416, tragic poets rarely competed at the Lenaea. It was a smaller, less prestigious celebration where the audience was likely to be composed only of local people.

The City, or Great, Dionysia took place in the spring at the end of March, in the Greek month of Elaphebolion, when the whole Hellenic world could travel to Athens. Thus the festival provided the occasion for the citizens to display their wealth, patriotism, and talent. The audience may have blessed the orphans of the city's war dead and inspected the tribute just brought in by the allies before watching the competitions for dithyrambs, tragedies, and comedies. The celebration began with an elaborate religious procession; a bull was sacrificed in the sacred precinct, bloodless offerings were made, participants in the performance paraded in elegant dress, and the cult statue of Dionysus himself was escorted to his own special seat next to his priest in the theater. During the war, at least three days of the festival were devoted to drama. On each day, five plays would be presented; three tragedies and a satyr play, called a tetralogy, all by one playwright, and then a comedy. As at the Lenaea, the performances were offered in competition, and the victors were announced at the completion of the last day.

The entire community participated in the production of the

plays. Some months after the end of the festivals, the *archon*, or public official, selected the dramas which would be presented at the next year's celebrations. Wealthy citizens were required to pay the expenses and oversee the production of one play. The poor may have even received a state subsidy to cover their own festival expenses such as seats in the theater. Judges chosen by lot, one from each of the ten tribes of citizens, decided which plays were best. The victorious poet was proclaimed in the theater and crowned with ivy while the audience cheered or booed their representatives' choice. At the end of the Great Dionysia the citizens held an assembly to investigate the conduct of the officials who were in charge of the festival.

Just who was this god Dionysus? And why should drama be a form of worshipping him? To call him the god of wine is too simple; wine itself has always been symbolic of much more. It is the sap that flows in plants, the blood that rushes through all living animals, the pulsating, liquid force of life itself.[7] Dionysus is a god of life—a fertility deity whose mythic death and rebirth connect him with the death and rebirth of all nature in the cycle of seasons. His association with the bull embodies the strength, violence, and irrationality in nature as well as its virility. But as the god of wine and revels, Dionysus is also the bearer of gifts which enable man to see into the mysteries of life. Wine is the great relaxer, the liberator from inhibition. In partnership with the frenzied beats of Dionysiac drums, cymbals, and dance, it releases revelers from themselves and from their sense of separateness and leads them to experience union with nature and to absorb its powers. Euripides' *Bacchae* reveals how barbaric Dionysus' rites must have been; the ecstatic worshippers who can fondle wild beasts are also capable of ripping apart living things and eating them raw.

The lesson of *Bacchae* is that Dionysus represents irrational forces which cannot be repressed without peril. But it is also clear that the community which would progress and submit to the rule of law must channel the vital energies represented by this god into a less destructive form of worship. This may have been one of the motives that led to the establishment of the City Dionysia in 536 B.C. What better way to both control and satisfy the people than by state supervision of processions, sacrifice, music, even revels, and, most important, public spectacles? Here ordinary citizens in masks transform themselves to reenact that moment when even the most powerful hero confronts his own mortality. Here the audience too, participating vicariously through its identification with both chorus and protagonist, becomes engrossed in the action and discharges the anxieties that demand release. The spectators experience the hero's defeat, as inevitable as the coming of winter, and yet leave the Theater of Dionysus renewed, assured by the festival as a whole, and certainly by the comedies, that spring can never be far behind, that there always exists the potential for human victory. Just as Apollo and Dionysus, gods of the rational and irrational in man, share the shrine at Delphi, so here in the dramatic festival the poles of man's life—birth and death, progress and destruction, triumph and limitation—are both recognized and revered.

III *Old Comedy*

Comedy as an art form came late to the festivals. The first official performance did not take place until 486 B.C. Certain elements of Aristophanic comedy, however, must be as old as the earliest worship of divinity. They derive from the *comos,* a carnival-like procession of revelers who sang and danced through town. Sometimes they led animals or wore animal costumes, and often they put on masks which simulated drunkenness. Many groups either wore or carried a huge phallus. Along the way, the participants engaged in banter with the bystanders, and their dirty jokes and insults provoked responses in kind. This type of humor has a ritual origin; obscenity and invective were believed to be powerful means of driving away evil spirits. In addition, these antics celebrated the vital forces in nature and insured the continued fertility of the land and its people.

From this joyous parade arose the chorus of Aristophanic comedy with its music and dance, its animal associations, and its formalized addresses to the audience. The religious origins also account for the extensive use of satire and obscenity. The things men blush at—farts and belches, erections and bosoms—and the things men fear—officials, institutions, and even gods—are permissible targets for ridicule in the comedies. Thus the play accomplishes the same sacred release as the wine and music of Dionysus the Liberator. The animal mummery, sexual license, and scatology also proclaim man's acceptance of his body and his unity with all nature. Ultimately, the exaltation of the physical is the highest form of worship of this fertility god. Moreover, as a celebration of man's union with immortal nature, comedy makes all things possible. It is the reverse of tragedy where the noble hero's own mortality dooms him to defeat. In comedy the hero is an ordinary man with ordinary virtues and vices. Yet when he attempts the impossible in the fantastic plots of comedy, he defeats all the forces, social and natural, which conspire to repress him. In several plays of Aristophanes, he even gets to heaven and triumphs over death itself.[8]

Somehow and at sometime the comos became a drama. It is difficult to explain the addition of actors to the chorus and the development of a plot with related episodes in dialogue rhythms rather than in lyric. Evidence comes from two sources—vase paintings and testimonials of the ancients.[9] Both indicate the popularity of improvised scenes from everyday life, many of which were probably obscene. Aristotle, however, attributes the invention of the comic plot to two Sicilian poets. But it is impossible to trace the way in which either the improvised scenes or the unified plots became the plays we have. According to Aristotle, comedy's earliest stages passed unnoticed in Athens because performances were put on by volunteers long before the archon granted a chorus to comic playwrights in 486 B.C.[10]

By the time comedy received official status, it had achieved a form unique enough to require the special term "Greek Old Comedy" to distinguish it from New Comedy familiar to us as the comedy of manners of Menander (342 - 290 B.C. in Athens), and Plautus and Terence (254 - 184 B.C. and 195 - 159 B.C. in Rome). Tragedy, which developed earlier, influenced several features of the structure of Old Comedy. Both kinds of drama begin with a prologue spoken by one or more actors to the audience or to each other. The chorus enters after the prologue, in the part known as the parodus. Both comic and tragic choruses marched on and sang their lines while dancing or moving their bodies in rhythm. Then, once the chorus has reached its place, its odes, now called stasima, alternate with the actors' scenes or episodes until the chorus leaves at the end of the play, in the exodus.

The speaking parts are distinguished from the choral parts by the type of verse as well as by the means of delivery.[11] Greek meter is quantitative, not accentual like English. Its pattern derives from the regular alternation of long (-) and short (u) syllables rather than of stressed (') and unstressed ones (-). It is most similar to English in the dialogue between actors because the Greek meter used for ordinary conversation is iambic trimeter. The basic pattern u-u-/u-u-/u-u- (similar to the -́-́-́-́-́ of iambic pentameter) is repeated line after line. Or, in more excited passages of dialogue, trochaic rhythms (*-u-u*, similar to the English '-'-) may appear, sometimes accompanied by a flute and declaimed or chanted rather than spoken. When the chorus converses with the actors, the chorus leader usually speaks for the whole group and uses dialogue rhythms.

The lyric meters of the chorus, however, have no natural English equivalents. They are made up of metrical phrases called *cola*. Many consist of irregular alternations of long and short syllables that cannot be divided into smaller units. There are many kinds of cola, with different lengths and movements, and they do not repeat themselves line after line, as does the meter in dialogue. Rather they occur in an infinite variety of combinations with other phrases to form unique lyric strophes. A choral lyric can be astrophic, or without responding parts, consist of several different paired strophes, or repeat only one strophe several times. If, in one ode, the rhythm of the strophe is repeated exactly, the second part of the pair is known as the antistrophe and the two are said to be in responsion. There is no evidence that the chorus actually divided in half to deliver the strophe and antistrophe separately. Sometimes the chorus and actors sing a lyric exchange, known as an amoebaean song. Or an actor himself may burst into a chant in lyric meter, called recitative, to express his heightened emotion. Since certain meters were specifically associated with the intense suffering characteristic of tragedy, Old Comedy frequently ridicules the high seriousness of tragedy by parodying its metrical peculiarities as well as its language and situations.

Old Comedy has several distinct features, the most obvious of which is its plot. First of all, the plot is invented and original, whereas tragedy and the satyr play are based on familiar myths. Secondly, the plot is fantastic; instead of presenting a "slice of life" with stock characters like New Comedy, the drama takes place in an unreal world such as Cloudcuckooland in the *Birds* or Hades in the *Frogs*. Even when the setting is realistic, the action allows the hero to accomplish the impossible, as when Dicaeopolis makes his private peace with Sparta in the *Acharnians*, or when *Lysistrata's* women, so helpless in real life, are able to end the Peloponnesian War. In any case, the reality of the situation is distorted in various ways to present a satiric comment on the institutions and attitudes of Athens.

Two other elements of Old Comedy, the agon or contest, and the parabasis (a direct address to the audience), may derive from the altercation and banter of the comos procession.[12] Both were certainly influenced, however, by the devices of rhetoric and the debate procedures of the assembly and law courts of fifth-century Athens.[13] The agon is a stylized argument between two contestants. Usually they quarrel and almost come to blows before the chorus separates them and sets up rules for the formal debate. Each of the contestants, called on by the chorus in turn, in an ode and antode, defends his position in a long speech (epirrheme and antepirrheme) and interrupts the other's with insulting comments that provoke similar responses. Several of Aristophanes' plays, however, contain only parts of this structure.

The parabasis, too, has a formal scheme and aims at persuasion. But unlike the agon, it is presented by the chorus alone and is directed toward the audience. Often it is totally unrelated to the rest of the drama and to the character and viewpoint that the chorus has previously assumed. Although not every play exhibits the full form, the complete parabasis contains seven parts. In the first, known as the commation, the chorus sends the actors away and comes forward to introduce the set piece to the audience. The second part is the parabasis proper, sometimes called the anapests after the meter most frequently used. Here the poet often expresses his own personal views, usually in an attempt to persuade the spectators that he and his production are worthy of the first prize or to offer, in seriousness or in jest, solutions to the city's problems. This section ends with the *pnigos* ("choking"), evidently because it was to be delivered in one breath at top speed.

The next part is known as an epirrhematic syzygy and is composed of a responding ode and antode sung in lyric meters and an epirrheme and antepirrheme usually recited in trochaic tetrameters. Here the chorus either remains outside the logical confines of the drama, reassumes its earlier role, or shifts back and forth between the two viewpoints. The lyrics often have religious associations, whereas the recited speeches contain lampoons, invective, and more advice. Since the commation occasionally instructs the chorus to disrobe or disarm, the anapests which follow may have been accompanied by lively dancing. Or it could have been the point where the choruses revealed their elaborate costumes.[14]

Comic plots lack the unity Aristotle judged best for tragedy. Most are not so perfectly constructed that nothing can be added, taken away, or rearranged without destroying the balance. Nor is any element of surprise or suspense sustained until the end. Rather an Old Comedy usually resolves its conflict early in the play and permits formalized interruptions like the agon and the parabasis as well as loosely connected episodes illustrating the success of the comic resolution. To many scholars this disorganization reveals the forced marriage of the brief improvised scenes to the comos at some earlier stage of comedy's development. Others find traces of the original fertility ritual of combat, victory, and sacred marriage in the episodic contests between the hero and his opponents and in the festivities which usually end the play.[15]

Critics used to consider the structure of Old Comedy unsophisticated and inferior because each scene does not lead to the next according to the laws of cause and effect. But comedy is not an imitation of a universal action designed to create a catharsis of pity and fear. Primarily it is produced to make people laugh. The disruption of the illusion of reality through various means is one of the major sources of its humor. This disruption serves also, by undermining the logical development, to dispel, at least briefly, the consciousness of the laws of probability and necessity which ordinarily limit man's actions and oppress his psyche. As Old Comedy's purpose is different, so is its form. It should not be compared to tragedy or the realistic plays of modern drama. Rather, it is more like a review, musical comedy, or the epic theater of Brecht.

IV *Production*

To visualize the performance, one must consider the theatrical conditions. Although the Theater of Dionysus can be seen in Athens today, most of the ruins at the foot of the Acropolis are at least half a century later than the time when Aristophanes' plays were first performed. Nor do the vase paintings, comments of later writers, and the information from the plays themselves clear up the many questions about the original production.[16] The main features of the theater can be described, however. The most important part was the orchestra, a circular space where the chorus danced, once they had entered from the wings. The audience sat in concentric rows of seats that encircled half of the orchestra and rose up the mountain slope. They faced a building known as a *skene* which probably contained the costumes and props needed for the performance. The facade of the skene formed a backdrop for the action. It was pierced by two or three doors, which usually represented entrances to private houses or the front of a palace. Through these doors the actors entered and exited into the playing area, which represented the street or a public place. The roof of the skene building and perhaps its upper-story windows could also be used for staging scenes. Movable sets or screens, painted to suggest different backgrounds, may have been put up in front of the doors for certain plays where the action does not take place near a palace or house. It is conjectured that the space directly in front of the skene was raised slightly, perhaps two or three steps above the orchestra, but it is also clear that this "stage" did not cut off free movement between the actors' and the chorus' levels.

Two mechanical devices certainly were used for the production. Actors portraying gods and heroes flew through the air and into the playing area suspended from a rope that was attached to a crane on the roof of the skene. Derived from the use of this "machine" in tragedy is the term *deus ex machina* to describe a plot resolved by the sudden appearance of a god. The other device, a low platform on wheels, called an ekkyklema, was rolled out from the central door of the skene so that the audience could see an interior scene. In tragedy, the ekkyklema was used most often to exhibit the bodies of the crazed or dead after the disaster had already occurred within. Aristophanes, mocking their use of this device, rolled out the tragedians themselves. It is not clear whether, at this early date, there were machines to produce sound effects like thunder. Hand props, such as pots and pans, and larger items like furniture or funeral biers are mentioned in the text and were probably used by the actors and the chorus.

Work on the production began about six months before the festival. Poets with plays to submit applied for a chorus from a government official who would then select the necessary number. It is clear from *Frogs* (1. 367) that comic poets received some money for their labor, but there is no further information about the amount. Nor is it known whether the victor received any more than an ivy crown when the prizes were awarded. The playwright could be his own producer or give his play to someone else to produce, as Aristophanes often did. Although actors were assigned by lot to the poet and paid for by the state itself, a sponsor was appointed from the rolls of wealthy citizens to outfit, train, and pay the chorus.

The chorus of Old Comedy contained twenty-four members. As the titles of Aristophanes' plays suggest, they often portrayed animals, birds, or fish, dressed in elaborate costumes with fancy masks to match. Sifakis conjectures that the audience eagerly anticipated and judged the ingenuity of the disguises.[17] How the chorus moved as they sang their odes is unclear, for rhythmic gestures of the hands and trunks would be enough to constitute "dance" in Greek terms. They surely imitated the movements of the animals they represented, but, in addition, we know they kicked high in the air, leaped, slapped their bodies, and spun like tops. The *kordax,* the characteristic dance to the flute, was particularly lascivious; the chorus members rotated their bellies and buttocks while keeping their feet close together.[18]

The actors were all male and were professionals paid by the state. In practice, the number of actors used in any one performance was limited to three. This meant that no more than three characters could engage in dialogue at any one time. But an actor could portray any number of roles in the same play. The First Actor portrayed the principal character who remained before the audience for most of the drama and interacted with the chorus. In scenes involving a second character, the Second Actor played the other major speaking parts. Between his exits and entrances, he changed his mask and role inside the skene building. If three characters appeared together in single sections of dialogue, a Third Actor was required to fill all the minor speaking roles. Some comedies, however, seem to demand a fourth actor as well.[19] But there was no limit on the number of silent extras that could appear. Aristophanes' plays abound with parts for supernumeraries such as slaves, children, and beautiful dancing girls.

Costumes were an important element of the production. Actors portraying males wore a pair of tights with a large leather phallus attached. A short chiton, or tunic, worn over this would leave the phallus still visible. To portray a woman or to mock a hero of tragedy an actor would wear a long robe. It is not clear how the actors who played naked women were costumed; perhaps pubic hair was attached to their tights instead of the phallus. Nor is it clear whether actors wore special padding at this time. They did wear masks with large openings for the mouth and eyes. Those who portrayed living persons like Socrates may have had masks that were recognizable caricatures. In the *Knights* Aristophanes apologizes for the Paphlagonian's mask, saying none of the maskmakers dared to produce a portrait of Cleon. Surely the maskmakers were free to use their imaginations to portray the fantastic characters of Old Comedy, like the Hoopoe's servant in *Birds* or the one-eyed ambassador of *Acharnians.*

Since the masks precluded any use of facial expression in portraying character or emotion, the actor's voice and body were extremely important. To some extent, his words tell us how he feels: "I weep," "I laugh," "I defecate from fear." But clearly he must have used his arms and the trunk of his body more than modern actors do. He probably knelt, prostrated himself and moved rapidly around the playing area to increase the range of his expression. We know the audience appreciated good acting; contests for actors were held at the Lenaea as early as 442 B.C., and Aristophanes mocked one (*Frogs* l. 303) who had mispronounced a line of Euripides.

The plays were performed outdoors with no curtain and hardly any stage or set. Thus, there could be no attempt at realism. The playwright, producer, and actors must have depended on the audience's acquiescence to certain established conventions. Time and place were revealed primarily through the words of the actors and chorus. Hand props like a torch or a lantern could also be used to indicate darkness. An altar on the stage might represent anything from a tomb to a shrine. Stage hands who wheeled forward the ekkyklema or carried large props in and out were ignored, while the exhibition of intimate scenes outside of the house was accepted as natural.

The use of a limited number of actors, wearing masks and phalluses, and the presence of a fantastically dressed chorus presuppose that the audience would not expect realistic drama where the illusion of actual life is created and sustained. Instead, Old Comedy presents a fractured view of reality and moves in and out of fantasy, using the building and shattering of dramatic illusion as one of its major devices for humor, satire, and sacred release. It both accepts and mocks the conventions of dramatic performance and thus makes its own affectations one of its targets for satire. It keeps the audience aware that a performance is going on and even makes them part of it through direct address, and by lampooning or portraying the very citizens who are watching them.

The composition and sophistication of the audience are still open questions.[20] The theater accommodated about fourteen thousand people, a much larger group than attend our dramatic performances. Women and children, both slaves and free, were probably allowed to see Old Comedy with all its obscenities. Perhaps they sat or stood in the back, however. The front rows seem to have been reserved for dignitaries such as priests, government officials, public benefactors, and foreign ambassadors. Since the people sat on the hard stone seats from dawn until dusk, they probably brought food from home as well as soft cushions.

Anecdotes about audience reaction—tears at the tragedy *Capture of Miletus*, horror at the masks of the Eumenides—suggest interest and involvement, but it is hard to determine how much was understood. It is clear that a great deal of the humor of Old Comedy was designed for a popular rather than an elite audience. As *Clouds'* parabasis reveals, the comedians were fiercely competitive and used all the devices they could to win a first prize. The stock jokes, pantomime, and obscenity would please the lowest level. The topical allusions and satire of familiar places, people, and events would also evoke laughter from fellow Athenians. The question of how seriously Aristophanes meant, and the audience took, the satire is debatable and must be considered play by play. But the nature of Old Comedy demands the temporary destruction of all institutions and individuals that restrict man's freedom or that insist upon being taken seriously. Therefore, because the audience demanded it, Aristophanes had to attack the most obvious targets, the rich, the powerful, and the intellectual elite, regardless of his own convictions.

Parodies of tragedy or contemporary science and philosophy demand little precise knowledge. The incongruity of familiar tragic style and language in a comic situation is enough by itself to make the audience laugh. When the affectations of the learned quack, with his pretentious jargon and mannerisms, are exposed by the simple fool, we confront a basic ingredient of comedy that goes all the way back to the earliest improvised scenes. The joke is much funnier, of course, to those who recognize the exact lines being parodied, understand the subtleties of meter and diction, and know the thinkers as well as their thoughts. But the humor is not directed toward these sophisticates alone. It is successful because the entire audience shares the same general culture and expectations about the performance.

CHAPTER 2

War and Peace: Acharnians (Akharnēs *and* Peace (Eirēnē)

I *Summary of* Acharnians

THE *Acharnians*, which won first prize at the Lenaea of 425, reflects conditions in Athens during the sixth year of the Peloponnesian War. Pericles' war strategy was to defeat the enemy quickly by maintaining control of the seas without risking a land battle with the superior Spartan army. In effect, the area outside Athens was abandoned to the enemy. For the past six summers, all the farmers of Attica had retreated within the city walls to watch as the Spartan invaders ravaged their fields. They suffered as much from the expense and discomfort of city life as from the loss of their crops. But by 425 Pericles was dead, and unfortunately for the refugees, the war dragged on with no end in sight.

Dicaeopolis, the hero of the *Acharnians*, is just such a refugee. In the prologue the old farmer laments his changed life while he waits for the assembly to meet. His hopes for a serious discussion of peace are quickly smashed when Amphitheus is ejected from the meeting for raising the subject. Instead the citizens hear reports from freeloading ambassadors who waste time and public money in foreign courts. Disappointed and disgusted, Dicaeopolis allows Amphitheus to arrange a private thirty-year truce with Sparta. He receives his treaty in the form of a full wineskin. As the farmer prepares to celebrate, however, he is attacked by old men from the Athenian district of Acharnae. These once valiant warriors who have been dispossessed by the Spartans fiercely hate anyone who would negotiate with the enemy. Dicaeopolis forces them to stop stoning him by seizing a hostage. Once he has borrowed a costume and confidence from Euripides, he speaks with his head in a chopping block to persuade the Acharnians that his truce is sensible and patriotic.

30

His arguments convince half the chorus, but the rest call out Lamachus, the general, to answer him. Although Lamachus is defeated, he refuses to concede and goes into his house vowing eternal war with Sparta. In revenge, Dicaeopolis announces that he will ban Lamachus from the market he is planning to open.

After the actors exit, the chorus performs the parabasis in which they defend the reputation of their poet, sing a hymn to the Muse of Acharnae, and describe the plight of old men harassed by lawsuits. Dicaeopolis then comes out to open his market. The episodes which follow illustrate his success. First he is able to buy the daughters of a starving Megarian for a bit of garlic and salt. Next he trades a despised Athenian informer for that most beloved of all delicacies—Boeotian eels. As Dicaeopolis cooks himself a lavish meal, the chorus looks on enviously. But the farmer refuses to share with them or with the poor cowherd and wedding guest who come to plead for a drop from his wineskin of peace. He relents and gives up a little to an excited bride just before two heralds arrive, one summoning Lamachus to war, the other inviting Dicaeopolis to a party. The two men trade insults as they prepare for their opposite destinations. After they leave, the chorus lampoons a sponsor who has refused them dinner. Then Lamachus is carried in wounded and groaning, while Dicaeopolis dances in supported by two courtesans. Cries of pleasure and pain alternate as one goes to the doctor and the other leads the chorus off singing a victory song because he has won a drinking prize.

II   *Public Conflict and Private Resolution*

As he waits alone for the assembly to begin, Dicaeopolis, whose name means "Just City," weighs the pleasures and pains of life as a refugee. The sorrows predominate—bad tragedy, bad music, bad government, and, worst of all, the Athenian marketplace crammed with sellers noisily hawking their wares. He looks tooward his own generous fields, longing for peace, but complains that most citizens don't care enough about it to attend the assembly. In his soliloquy, Dicaeopolis introduces several themes and objects of satire. The contrast between war and peace, which Aristophanes identifies with pain and pleasure, is the major antithesis around which the play is structured. The satire attacks the corruption of politicians, the inefficiency of government, the degeneration of poetry, and the materialism of urban life.

The assault on the government begins as soon as the assembly convenes. The citizens refuse even to hear the word "peace." Amphitheus is kicked out when he claims that the gods have sent him to negotiate with Sparta, and Dicaeopolis himself is shouted down as he tries to support him. Instead, the assembly is eager for reports from diplomats sent to exotic lands to get funds and supplies for war. The government is revealed as slow, stupid, and corrupt. Ambassadors have spent eleven years feasting in Persia while poor soldiers and sailors endure all the hardships of war. Even so, the ambassadors have not accomplished their task. The King's Great Eye attends the assembly wearing a mask with one large eye and bearing a name, Shambyses (Douglass Parker's translation), to imply duplicity. Through double-talk he avoids promising that the Great King will lend Athens gold, and his eunuchs turn out to be more Athenians on the take. The scene lampoons the Persians for the ostentatious size and wealth of their empire, for their inability to speak Greek, and for their vicious policy of dangling money before Athens and Sparta without committing themselves to help either side. But it is clear that most Athenians are gullible and that certain men are clever enough to profit from it.

When these swindlers go off to dine at public expense, they are replaced by another group. Their excuses for lingering in Thrace satirize Athens' barbarian allies who inhabit a frozen wasteland and who worship and emulate everything Athenian. The shortsighted ambassadors have brought back a troop of Odomantians, the most bloodthirsty of Thracians, whose fierceness is manifest in their enormous, redtipped phalluses. Although they have been hired to attack Boeotia, they attack Dicaeopolis instead as the terrified citizens stand by helplessly. The reality behind the comic exaggeration is clear. The Athenians were so fearful that their ally Sitacles would keep for himself what he captured for Athens that they eventually stopped sending aid to his troops. Moreover, mercenaries could easily turn on Athens, as occurred later in the war in Boeotia.

The scene also dramatizes how powerless the individual is against the government. But this is comedy where the hero will not allow himself to be silenced and oppressed. Dicaeopolis has already sent the ejected Amphitheus to Sparta to arrange a private peace. He returns with three truces in wineskins for Dicaeopolis to choose from. This identification of wine and peace connects Dionysus, the god of the festival, directly with the action and runs throughout the entire play. It arises from the fact that the Greek word for treaty, *sponde*, is the same as the word for the libation performed with wine. Once Dicaeopolis has selected the thirty-year vintage, all the delights associated with the vineyard—freedom, fertility, power, and pleasure—become the delights of peace. The chorus personifies peace as a nubile maiden, the companion of Aphrodite and Eros, who inhabits flourishing fields. When Dicaeopolis invokes Phales, the spirit of the phallus, as his drinking companion at the rural Dionysia, he describes the playful violence of sex. War, on the other hand, is personified as a destructive drunkard who brutally beats men and burns vines. But his representative, General Lamachus, is defeated by a vine stake, the instrument of peace, and Dicaeopolis earns the victory song for conquerors by winning a drinking bout at the feast for blessing the new wine.

Dicaeopolis barely has time to enjoy his thirty-year vintage when the chorus of poor old farmers and charcoal sellers from Acharnae rushes into the orchestra singing the parodus. As members of a valiant generation who defeated Persia, and as citizens whose vines have been devastated by Sparta, they are rabid opponents of peace. Thus in fury they have roused their feeble bodies to search for the traitor. When they catch Dicaeopolis peacefully celebrating a country feast of Dionysus, they angrily pelt him with stones. But Dicaeopolis seizes a hostage, a basket of coals, to force them to hear his defense. The old men yield immediately, for that basket, containing their only means of livelihood, is like a beloved fellow demesman to them. In fact, the coals are the Acharnians, fierce, sputtering, and always threatening violence. Once the men have been convinced by Dicaeopolis, however, the coals are converted to peaceful, life-sustaining purposes: they are used by Dicaeopolis for cooking epicurean delights.

When Dicaeopolis seizes the basket of coals, he initiates a parody of Euripides' tragedy *Telephus*.[1] That hero used a threat to the infant Orestes to force the leaders of the Trojan War to hear his arguments against fighting for the sake of a woman. Now, with tragic bravado, Dicaeopolis stakes his life on his ability to persuade the Acharnians that their war is equally senseless. Once the chorus stops stoning him, he goes to the house of Euripides to borrow the ragged costume of Telephus to arouse the pity and interest of his judges. Euripides' slave announces that the tragedian is at home and not at home; his mind is off gathering verses while his body is making a tragedy. Euripides finally agrees to be rolled out on the ekkyklema and impatiently offers help. Dicaeopolis wants more than the tattered robe of Telephus, however; first he begs a hat, then a staff, a broken cup, a pot, and finally some herbs. Euripides' lame protests are defeated by Dicaeopolis' persistence. The tragedian is rolled back indoors complaning that Dicaeopolis has destroyed his plays by removing all the special effects.

The parody performs several functions. First of all, it ridicules the intellectual pretensions of both the dramatists and the patrons of drama. When the old country bumpkin manages to filch most of the prop room, he deflates the arrogance of the tragedian and his slave. But the pretensions of tragedy are targets as well. The grand paradoxes of human limitation and potential are reduced to such ridiculous antinomies as "at home and not at home." The audience's catharsis comes not from character or action but from the pitiful costumes and props or the ekkyklema's grim spectacle. Yet Dicaeopolis intends to use these very devices to appeal to his audience. In addition, as Dicaeopolis puts on the clothes, he assumes the mannerisms of the tragic hero. He punctuates his speeches with tragic exclamations like: "Oh Zeus! Oh my Soul! Oh wretched me!" More important, he has drunk down Euripides (l. 486). That is, he has absorbed the rhetorical skills needed to win his case and has assumed a grandeur which elevates both him and his subject. A veritable Telephus, he heroically approaches his captors.

In the agon, Dicaeopolis pleads his case from a chopping block, the low comic or kitchen equivalent of a noose, for he will die a traitor if he cannot win. Addressing the spectators as well as the chorus, he states his impeccable credentials as a Sparta-hater whose vines have also been cut. But, instead of blaming the Spartans for all the trouble, he acknowledges that they have legitimate complaints against the Athenians. His analysis of the causes of the war belongs to the world of comedy. It parodies the mythology of the Trojan War (the subject of Telephus' plea) as well as Herodotus' introduction to his *Histories*. When the Megarians kidnapped two whores from the house of Pericles' mistress, Pericles excluded Megara from the markets of Athens and her empire. On behalf of the starving Megarians, the Spartans began the fighting. Dicaeopolis accuses both sides of overreacting and then senselessly delighting in the preparations for war. By identifying Megara, the victim of a real economic boycott, as the chief source of comic contention, Aristophanes develops the themes of the crassness of the Athenian marketplace and the deprivation that war necessitates.

Half the chorus is persuaded by this mixture of nonsense and

serious criticism. Its leader congratulates Dicaeopolis, but the unconvinced call on Lamachus to come out and defend the war, just as
Achilles was summoned to debate Telephus. The real Lamachus
was elected general several times, participated in the peace
negotiations of 421, and was killed in battle in 414 while sharing the
command of the Sicilian expedition. Aristophanes probably chose
him to represent the supporters of the war because his name contains the word for battle (*machē*). Here he portrays the braggart
soldier, armed head to toe, wearing a fearful crested helmet, and
bearing a Gorgon's shield. Although Lamachus threatens and insults, the old farmer again deflates his superior's pretensions by
reducing the symbols of his greatness. Terrified by his costume,
Dicaeopolis first literally disarms the general of his shield, and then
borrows a feather from his helmet ("from the braggart bird?"
Dicaeopolis asks) to help him vomit up his fright. Later, when
Lamachus is wounded, the loss of his gorgon and great plume symbolizes his defeat. In the grandiloquent language of tragedy, the
warrior relates their loss to his own death. The rustic also outwits
the general with his brash accusation that the young and rich take
the soft jobs for good pay while the poor old citizens fight the war.
This argument convinces the chorus, but not Lamachus, who
retreats into his house swearing eternal war with Sparta while
Dicaeopolis exits after barring the warrior from the market he is
about to open.

Now that the actors have withdrawn through the doors in the
scene building, the chorus is alone in the orchestra and comes
forward to perform the parabasis, their direct address to the
audience. In the anapests, or parabasis proper, the leader defends
the poet against charges that he has slandered the city and its people. Thus, although there are no direct references to the drama, the
poet has placed himself in the same position as his hero, for both
must prove their honesty, courage, and patriotism to a hostile
audience. Dicaeopolis has already identified himself with
Aristophanes by referring to Cleon's attack for slander. (ll. 377 - 82)
and by setting the chopping-block scene at the Lenaea (ll. 502 - 4).
By extension, the audience is drawn into the drama to share the role
of his Acharnian judges. The chorus initiates this by asking them for
help in finding the traitors. Dicaeopolis then pleads with the Acharnians as if they were the entire Athenian citizenry gathered together
at the festival of Dionysus (ll. 505 - 7). Later, while awaiting
Lamachus, the part of the chorus that remains unconvinced appeals

for help from any general or soldier in the audience. In the parabasis, the leader develops the relation. He proves how much the poet's frankness has enlarged the reputation of Athens and increased the chances for peace by impressing the allies, the Persians, and even the enemy with the value of free speech and the strength of democracy. Once the entire chorus has been persuaded by Dicaeopolis, the spectators can transfer their goodwill from him to the poet. Aristophanes has been clever enough to flatter the citizens for their liberality while proving his honesty at their expense.

For the rest of the parabasis the chorus returns to the role of Archarnians to describe their plight as old men confounded by lawsuits that leave them humiliated, speechless, and bankrupt. This section, in effect, identifies them, and, by extension, the spectators, with the powerless Dicaeopolis of the prologue. Now that they see themselves in his position, they can take vicarious pleasure in his success although (or perhaps because) he refuses to share it.

III   *Peace and Prosperity*

As the chorus completes the parabasis, Dicaeopolis emerges to open his market and announces the rules. In place of the Athenian market overseer, he introduces a three-pronged whip, a substitution representing the arbitrary rules which oppress the poor. Like Pericles, Dicaeopolis has decreed that his own enemy, Lamachus, be excluded from the market. But he also bans informers, loud-mouths, and troublemakers, so that, according to a later ode, one can trade there undisturbed even by bad poets (ll. 836 - 59). The chorus is so enthusiastic that Douglass Parker thinks it was singing directly to the audience, and attempting to attract them as customers to the market.[2]

Two episodes illustrate the increasing commercial success of Dicaeopolis. In the first, a starving Megarian tries to sell his two daughters as sacrificial piglets. The very outrageousness of the ruse transforms the Megarian's desperation into comedy. The humor also depends on the double meaning of the word *choiros*—pig and vagina—which associates peace with good food and sex. The bargaining is full of puns and obscenities as the men examine the girls' bodies and discuss their impending sacrifice to Aphrodite. After the choral ode, a rich merchant arrives from Boeotia with a stock of gastronomic treats. Now Dicaepolis can fill up on his beloved Boeotian eels of which the war had deprived him. Again the humor arises from an outlandish act. When the Boeotian wants to be paid with something uniquely Athenian, Dicaeopolis satisfies him with an informer whom he wraps up like a vase produced and packaged for export. Dicaeopolis has proved his skill as a salesman, for he has exchanged a detestable product for a prized delicacy. In addition, he has outsmarted the Boeotians whose gluttony and dull wits were proverbial.

His prosperity convinces the chorus that they have all had enough of war. They now know peace can bestow everything good, even the erotic pleasures of youth. The episode which follows indicates that Dicaeopolis has convinced others as well. The poor blind farmer and the wedding guest who beg for a drop of his peace wine represent a society ready to renounce war. The fact that Dicaeopolis shares his peace with the bridegroom who has been drafted symbolizes the triumph of the life-force celebrated in comedy. When he prescribes how the bride should apply the balm, he connects peace with Phales, and, thus, with Dionysus himself.

But another facet of Dicaeopolis' victory is illustrated in the same episode. While the chorus looks on enviously, he prepares a sumptuous meal for his family and taunts his hungry observers. Nor will he share his peace with the ruined farmer, or the gift-bearing wedding guest. He bestows his gift on the bride only because he sympathizes with her sexual needs, not because of any altruistic principle. The chorus reacts to his selfishness in a lampoon at the end of the episode (ll. 1150 - 72) when they pray that the sponsor who cheated them out of dinner be forced to watch a feast cooked and not be allowed to share it.

In the same episode, Dicaeopolis is personally invited to the Feast of the New Wine by a priest of Dionysus, while Lamachus is summoned to guard the borders against invasion. Here and in the final episode the defeat of the general and the forces of war is reflected in the imagery. The two neighbors make their preparations and live out their different destinies side by side, but in tones which underline the contrast between war and peace. The foods they prepare represent the deprivations of war (that is, onions and salt meat) as opposed to the prosperity of peace (that is, thrushes and pigeons). As Lamachus gathers together the weapons of death (spear, round-buckler), his neighbor calls for objects which look similar but are life-sustaining (skewer, round cheesecake). The general grandly puts on full armor, but Dicaeopolis boasts that his drinking cup is all he needs. And he is right. In the final episode, a vine stake wounds the general, and victory in a drinking contest turns the reveler into a hero.

The contrast between war and peace in the final episodes is further emphasized by the contrast between the comic and the tragic style. The herald who summons Lamachus to duty introduces the parody of tragic diction and rhythms.[3] Lamachus himself laments his assignment in the grand style, arms himself with heroic bravado, and then bewails his defeat with the eloquence and emotion of a tragic hero. The description of his fall is delivered by a messenger in the typically tragic manner. But his passion is rendered ludicrous by the comic actions which Dicaeopolis performs at the same time.

IV   *The Meaning of the Victory*

It is difficult to prove that *Acharnians* is dramatizing the position of a peace party. Although peace and the poor farmer triumph in the play, war was a fact of life in the ancient world, and there was no serious peace movement in Athens at this early date because neither side had gained or suffered enough. The justice of the Peloponnesian War as a whole is not seriously questioned. Its origins are reduced to nonsense in Dicaeopolis' plea. Only the Megarian Decree is taken seriously as a major cause (although Thucydides barely mentions it). Its importance here is thematic rather than political. War takes away the basic joys of life. The starving Megarian demonstrates how far one will go for garlic and salt. Nor does the character of the warmonger bear much resemblance to the historical general, Lamachus. Instead, he is a stock comic figure, the braggart soldier, whose affectations are revealed by the coward. Moreover, when Dicaeopolis concludes his private peace, he keeps it to himself and his family. Thus, the play does not offer any serious political indictment or provide a patriotic model.

The hardship of war is only one of the problems of real life that the comedy selects for exaggeration and distortion. Dicaeopolis and the Acharnians are old and poor whereas Lamachus and the men who monopolize the safe jobs and control all the money are young and strong. The decrepitude, powerlessness, and sense of loss which old age inevitably brings are all dramatized here. So too is the bitterness of poverty—from Dicaeopolis' opening complaints about the noisy market to the visits of the Megarian and the blind

cowherd. The government, which victimizes in the name of protection, oppresses the citizenry at all levels, from the most crucial
aspects of public affairs (the scene at the assembly) to the common
occurrences of daily life (references to lawsuits and informers).

But comedy takes real life and distorts it to deprive it, for the moment at least, of the seriousness that human beings attach to it. The
comic situation may derive from facts, but Aristophanes' theatrical
translation of them is sheer fantasy. Poor, old, and powerless
Dicaepolis manages to get control over all the forces that restrain
him, including old age itself, as is proved by his ability to satisfy the
girls while drunk. The Persian and Thracian foreigners, the
Megarian piglets, and the informer packed up like a vessel with its
mouth stopped are transformed by means of sight gags, dialect
jokes, puns, and parodies into metaphors that create a new reality
and dispel the threats of the old.[4] The audience is unable to take the
comedy itself seriously because actors and chorus move in and out
of the drama, often speaking directly to the spectators. The poet
even interrupts the action just for the sake of developing a joke such
as the piglet / vagina pun or the resemblance of the Great Eye of
Persia to the eye painted on Greek ships. Dover suggests that the
disruption of the dramatic illusion, which he calls "discontinuity of
characterization," provides great freedom for the characters to say
whatever they please. Thoughts which would puzzle or anger if expressed in real life or realistic drama, erupt in the comic dialogue
without evoking the expected response.[5]

Freedom is really the key word in Old Comedy. The hero of the
Acharnians finds himself in a dismal situation—poor, old, repressed,
and cheated. But Dicaeopolis rises above individual opponents,
society, and even forces of nature. The dramatic structure is unified
not by the laws of probability and necessity but by the theme of the
hero's self-assertion.[6] One by one, Dicaeopolis defeats all the forces
which would destroy his physical and psychological well-being. He
turns aside the violence of the government and the Acharnians. He
defeats the intellectual pretensions of the poets and bravado of the
generals. He sets up his own market where he himself becomes the
salesman he once despised. The episodes which illustrate his growing success demonstrate a further element of self-assertion.
Dicaeopolis has succeeded for himself alone, with no thought of
public weal or private pity. By the end, he has become the individual par excellence, the reverse of the poor powerless farmer of
the prologue and, indeed, hardly different from the powers that

once held him down. He uses force to drive the undesirables out of
his market, profits from the starving Megarian, and flaunts his
goods before the envious chorus and unhappy general.

The growth of his power is accompanied by an increase in sexual
allusion. Obscenity is, of course, ubiquitous in *Acharnians* as in
other Old Comedies.[7] In part, Dover points out, sex jokes and
vulgar language "cap . . . or bring a passage to a climax, after
which the prolonged laughter of the audience enables the subject to
be broken off and a fresh line of dialogue to be started."[8] The
emphasis on sex also punctures the serious man's assumption that
his mind is the most important element in his life. Obscenity
proclaims man's acceptance of his union with physical nature, symbolized by Dionysus. Moreover, it is a powerful means of self-
assertion, since neither the real words nor instinctive actions are
accepted in polite society. Dicaeopolis' sexuality develops from
allusions, wishes, and insults through the purchase of the piglets
and sympathy for the aroused bride up to its literal climax in the exodus when, drunk and potent, he leads two dancing girls away.
Now his self-assertion is complete. He has triumphed not only over
war and generals, but over sterile Old Age itself.

And what catharsis do the triumph and the comic reversal evoke?
Does the audience emerge with a desire to change governments or
policies because peace has been proved more fun than war? More
likely, the drama seems to enable the citizens to take their institutions and ideas less seriously. By making Dicaeopolis become
exactly what he has detested as an underdog, the comedy seems to
demonstrate that certain conditions are in the nature of things.
Thus, comic distortion leads the audience back to the acceptance of
real life and the worship of all that Dionysus represents.

V *Variations on the Theme:* Peace

By 421, when *Peace* was performed, conditions in Athens had
changed. The opposing generals had both been killed the summer
before at the battle of Amphipolis. Now that they could no longer
sabotage efforts to end the war, prospects for peace increased. The
peace party was growing in strength while Aristophanes was com-
posing the play, and the treaty itself, the Peace of Nicias, was for-
mally concluded only ten days after its performance. Von Daele
suggests that it may have even affected the outcome of the
negotiations.[9] Indeed, *Peace* euphorically celebrates the end of the

war with a subtle alteration in the spirit of Old Comedy. The play contains no agon. The formulaic fantasy emphasizes the heroic qualities of men, and the satire of states and individuals is gentle and good-natured. Above all, the invincible hero defeats war, not for himself alone, but for everyone, citizen and subject, friend and enemy. Unlike Dicaeopolis, he offers freedom, food, and sex to the whole Greek world in the grand finale which ends, like a Dionysiac comos, in a sacred marriage to the personification of peace.

Because the plot, characters, and even the parabasis resemble earlier plays, some scholars suspect that *Peace* was hastily composed to suit the fast-breaking events of that winter and spring.[10] The hero, Trygaeus, whose name comes from the word "crop," is a small farmer like the hero of *Acharnians*, Dicaeopolis. Thwarted in his attempts to promote peace through the system, Trygaeus also resolves to take matters into his own hands. Not by concluding a private truce, however. His fantasy is much grander. He is determined to get to Olympus to plead with Zeus himself. In a parody of a recent drama by Euripides, he soars up on a dung beetle, the comic equivalent of Pegasus, the winged horse whom the hero Bellerophon rode to heaven.[11] The beast's appetite for finely kneaded cakes of feces provides ample opportunity for scatological humor. His master's fear of the crane, tragedy's machine for ascents to Olympus, and his lyric declamations heighten the ludicrous disparity between the myth and its comic transformation. The two questers even get to heaven too late; Zeus and his Olympians have fled the noise of the war below, leaving Hermes behind, with War and Tumult in charge and Peace buried deep in the ground.

Undaunted by the dire warnings of Hermes, he hastens to dig her up, summoning the aid of the chorus of farmers and laborers who are ecstatic at the prospect of peace. They succeed in digging up not only the goddess herself, but her two beautiful companions Opora, "Harvest," and Theoria, "Sacred Embassy," the private and public gifts of Peace. Trygaeus is to marry the former, whereas the latter will be presented to the Athenian council. While he goes off to prepare the wedding feast, the chorus performs the parabasis. Then a series of episodic scenes demonstrates the hero's success. War profiteers who refuse to convert to peacetime industries are driven away. Grateful farmers enter to thank Trygaeus for restoring their livelihoods and their pleasures. The contrast between the simple delights of peace and the pain and propaganda of wartime also resembles *Acharnians*; again Lamachus appears as the symbol for the war party, despite the fact that he was one of the negotiators of the Peace of Nicias. The play ends with a joyously sensual wedding song, inviting all Greeks to share the promised benefits as well as the cakes. By the exodus, both the hero and the beast have surpassed their tragic models. The dung beetle has been harnessed to the chariot of Zeus, and Trygaeus has been truly apotheosized—made young again, wedded to a goddess with the promise of eternal fertility, and worshipped by all.

As the action progresses, the poet ridicules the pretense that war is a glorious endeavor. The scene on Olympus demolishes the epic vision that the gods value the heroics of men. The highest deities have become so disgusted by the human squabbles that they have fled heaven. War is personified as a gross blusterer whose vulgarity is symbolized by the noise and violence of his mortar and pestle. The supporters of the war are exposed as foolish politicians, greedy arms manufacturers, quack fortune-tellers, and ambitious soldiers. With typical comic distortion, Hermes explains that fear, honor, and self-interest, not political principles, have caused the war. Pericles began the whole thing by issuing the Megarian Decree to distract the people from blaming him for his friend Phidias' peculations. Once started, it could not be stopped, because of the same greed and ambition of rich and poor all over the Greek world.

The chorus of *Peace* is extremely friendly to Trygaeus and the city. It is made up of laborers and farmers from all over Greece who, instead of opposing the hero, slow him down at first by reacting too enthusiastically to his plan. Even those groups who are accused of shirking finally pull hard with the rest to haul Peace up. Moreover, neither they nor the actors engage in a real agon which might arouse rival parties by a debate, even humorous, of the pros and cons of peace. And the parabasis concentrates on poetry rather than politics. In the anapests, the chorus leader boasts of the poet's originality and public service. The emphasis on the courageous acts performed selflessly "for you and the isles" (ll. 759 - 60) subtly connects the poet with the hero of his play. The ode and antode, where lampoon is traditional, attack the new poets. The imagery picks up patterns from the rest of the play—monsters, gluttony, turds, stench, and tumult—but the targets are familiar and apolitical. Other choral odes, where one might expect particularized satire, instead contrast the pleasures of peace with the discomforts of war or attack hypocritical warmongers in general.

As Trygaeus defeats his enemies, Aristophanes emphatically establishes the meaning of his victory. Calling for help, the hero shouts, "Now the time has come for the song of Dates, sung while he masturbated at noon, 'Oh how I enjoy myself, how I delight, how good I feel.'" (ll. 289 - 291). In contrast to the pain of war, well-remembered by the chorus of workers, peace offers pleasure, joy in the simple acts of life—sex, eating, creative work, and music. So the goddess gives "Harvest" as a wife to "Crop." Thus pleasure and productivity are blended in all the references to marriage and farming. The language is full of double entendre, continually alluding to genitalia, the sex act, and its results. Public life too is directed toward joyous celebration. So "Sacred Embassy" replaces battle as the business of government when Theoria is presented to the entire council. She is undressed to be enjoyed in an exuberant extended metaphor of holiday games, complete with wrestling, riding, and racing. The obscenities contribute to the joie de vivre.

But the equation "peace is love" means more than public and private sex and fertility. It is extended to embrace the political concept of Panhellenism. Both the chorus and the hero alternately represent Athens and the entire Greek world. Hermes' analysis of the war focuses mainly on the plans and problems of the Athenian empire. Trygaeus sometimes seems limited to his own city. But from the beginning, he views himself as champion of all Greece (l. 93), and his call for help is addressed to the Hellenes at large (l. 292). Dover speculates that in the hauling scene the chorus has its back to the audience so that Trygaeus' summons seems to extend beyond the specifically Athenian "metics, [non-citizens who resided in Athens] foreigners, and islanders" (ll. 297 - 98) to the entire audience, nation, and even the world.[12] In fact, the spectators, representative of city and cosmos, have all participated in his quest, for they have held back their bowels until he could get the dung beetle off the ground. Once they have also helped with the digging, they are invited to share the benefits. Theoria is actually led to the members of the council, who were watching the performance from the front rows of the theater. When the characters make their offering to Peace, they scatter lustral water and barley on the audience. Trygaeus then prays that "Zeus mix us Hellenes again in the juice of friendship and harmony (ll. 996 ff.)." In the end, the final prayer for wealth and fertility is offered in the name of Hellenes (ll. 1320 ff.), and food and drink is shared with all as the wedding party marches off.

As Trygaeus liberates the goddess, Aristophanes changes the connotations of the imagery to underline the effects of peace. At the beginning, earthly existence is a disgusting cluster of sights, sounds, tastes, and smells symbolized, of course, by the dung beetle's meal of feces. So long as Trygaeus is on earth with his beetle and Peace is buried deep within it, the characters and audience are befouled. Trygaeus' waste supplies food for his beetle, whereas we too are potential feeders whose very farts might stimulate its appetite. The earth itself is full of cesspools and privies. But the beetle's demand for finely minced cakes promises his ascent to higher things. Once Peace is hauled out of her pit, the beetle will eat ambrosia among the gods while the people savor fragrant fruits, wines, and epicurean delights. The entire earth becomes redolent with the sweet odors of fecundity. The bad-food smells now belong specifically to the soldiers' life; freedom from the draft is like perfume, but the soldiers' kit stinks of belched onions (ll. 526 - 29). The reversal of the scatological images reaches its zenith when Trygaeus relegates the grandiose weaponry of war to the broom closets and outhouses of the city. The noise and activity demanded for the kneading of cakes is also picked up and developed. The violent pounding in the mortar of war becomes the gentle mixing in the drink of friendship when the individual ingredients are joined together as Hellenes. The tumult and squabble of war, so noisy it disturbed the gods, is converted to the uncontrollable dance of joy by the diggers and then finally to the happy wedding song. These images emphasize that peace can transform human character, replacing selfish competition with cooperation and generosity. Hopefully, the audience will also be transformed through their participation in the euphoric action.

VI   *Postscript:* Lysistrata

Peace was within Athens' reach, in fact as well as fantasy, in 421. By 411, however, the war had been resumed, Athens' fleet had been destroyed, the empire was in revolt, and the Spartan army was occupying part of Attica itself. Now that an honorable peace seemed impossible. Aristophanes approached the theme with a more fantastic plot and more generalized satire than in the two earlier plays. *Lysistrata* contains very few topical allusions or attacks on individuals. Instead, its plot arises from the eternal battle between men and women, its diction employs the universal language of sex, and its humor depends more on situations and sight gags than on lampoons. The enemy is male chauvinism in general, and the warriors of both sides are exposed as weak husbands overpowered by women's wiles. Thus Aristophanes dramatizes the last hope that Athenians and Spartans are really brothers under their armor and that peace is as natural as marriage.

CHAPTER 3

School for Life; Clouds (Nephelai)

I Summary

A FTER winning first prizes for *Acharnians* and *Knights*, Aristophanes produced *Clouds* at the Great Dionysia of 423. This time his target was philosophy in general and in particular the science, rhetoric, and ethics spread by the intellectuals who flocked to Athens from all parts of the Greek world. The public personality on whom he focused was Socrates, famous for his idiosyncracies as well as his love of wisdom. Although Aristophanes considered *Clouds* his cleverest comedy, the judges rejected it, awarding only a third prize. In the parabasis, the chorus leader, speaking for the poet, berates the audience for not recognizing a masterpiece. Thus it is clear that the text we have is a revised edition, but the content of the original version remains a mystery.[1] Scholars are left with several perplexing problems. Why did the audience dislike *Clouds*? Perhaps they were offended by the presentation of Socrates as a charlatan. Or were they so incensed at the iconoclastic teacher's success that Aristophanes tried to strengthen the Just Discourse's arguments and added the punishment of Socrates?[2] The best answer may be the playwright's own: his audience preferred the bawdy and the simpleminded.

The comedy begins with a monologue by Strepsiades, an old man sleepless with worry over his debts, incurred because of his son Phidippides' mania for horses. While he laments, his son dreams aloud of winning a race. The desperate father hits upon the scheme of enrolling his son in the school next door, called the Thoughtery, where, for a fee, he can learn to cheat his creditors. When the son refuses, unwilling to lose status and his elegant tan, Strepsiades sends him away. The old man determines to go to school himself, despite a mind and memory slowed by age. Upon arriving at the Thoughtery, he discovers that the pupils are engaged in all kinds of intellectual activity from natural science to metaphysics, while the master Socrates hangs in a basket so his mind won't be dragged down to earth as he contemplates the heavens. Socrates promises the old man success in his quest and offers the patronage of the chorus of Clouds, representatives of his new divinities Aether and the Whirlwind. After the Clouds' stately parodus, Socrates proves their divinity by showing how they, not Zeus, cause rain, thunder, and lightning. The Clouds themselves assure the old man of their powers in the windy and ambiguous art of rhetoric. Hopeful of becoming a successful rogue, Strepsiades enters the Thoughtery.

But Strepsiades is too old and stupid to grasp the subtleties of grammatical gender and quantitative meter that Socrates insists on teaching. Nor can the old man solve the practical problems his teacher poses. Thus, he convinces his son Phidippides of his ignorance and persuades him to study at the school instead. To determine which mentor the son will follow, he and Strepsiades hear a debate between the Just and the Unjust Discourses. They choose the latter because it offers the power to make the weaker argument appear the stronger. And the education is a complete success. Armed with new subtleties taught him by his son, Strepsiades drives away two creditors who come to collect their debts. But the victory banquet reveals the flaw in Strepsiades' scheme. Phidippides can also use the technique against his father. After an argument about music, he strikes the old man and then proves he was right to do it. Angry and repentant, Strepsiades burns down the school that has produced such a callous youth.

II *Progressive Education*

Aristophanes, in *Clouds*, returned to a subject he had treated before. *Banqueters*, his earliest play (427 B.C.), is no longer extant, but we know it concerned a father who brought up his two sons according to different principles. In the agon, the one with the traditional upbringing debated the brother who was educated by means of the newest theories. In *Clouds*, the poet concentrated on the new philosophy itself and shifted the conflict from the brothers to parent and child. The initial confrontation between father and son in the prologue introduces many of the antitheses around which the play is built. Phidippides' mother is a sophisticated lady of the city, rich, aristocratic, idle, pleasure-seeking, and full of lascivious tastes. In contrast, the father is from the country where man enjoys a simple life composed of hard work and the delights of nature. The son's name, Thrifty Son of Horse, reflects the parents' rivalry for his soul. Thus father and son symbolize the conflict between country and city, simplicity and sophistication, idleness and work, moral responsibility and hedonism.

The most important antithesis is, of course, the conflict between the old and the new. The son's rebellion against his father is simply in the nature of things. In the last quarter of the fifth century, however, it meant more than the eternal battle between the generations. An entire cultural tradition seemed to be at stake. Greek philosophers from Ionia and Sicily as well as the mainland were building on cosmologial speculations of the previous century, applying conclusions about natural phenomena to human nature and human institutions. The value of these studies can be seen in the medical writings of the Hippocratic school and in Thucydides' penetrating analysis of individual and collective motives for political acts. But other aspects threatened the stability of a society which was based on belief in the gods and universal justice. The conventions which had guided society, its laws, customs, and beliefs—known collectively as *nomos*—were generally accepted as divinely inspired. But the many conflicting theories about the origin and composition of the natural world led philosophers to skepticism. Protagoras, the traveling Sophist and friend of Pericles, believed that it was impossible to obtain knowledge about the gods. Instead he directed his attention to human problems, for he believed he could comprehend and control them by using his reason. In formulating the humanists' credo, "Man is the measure of all things," Protagoras suggested that the law, *(nomos)*, was relative and man-made, having changed as human needs changed. He never rejected *nomos*, however, as a useful tool for structuring man's life. Later Sophists, like Antiphon, the contemporary of Socrates, concentrated on studying nature *(physis)* and considered man part of the biological continuum, subject to physical and emotional needs too strong to be constrained by artificial conventions. For Antiphon, enlightened hedonism, not moral sanction, prevented anarchy. He believed one had to obey the law only if he were in danger of getting caught.[3] Thus in 423 the conflict between the old and the new contained within it the antithesis between *nomos*, with its conventional assumptions about moral absolutes, and *physis*, the new understanding of nature and its amoral government of human life.

Strepsiades reveals the common man's perception of the new philosophy: for a fee, you can learn how to win lawsuits even if you're in the wrong. And indeed, the Sophists did concentrate on the pragmatic goal of helping man to achieve a successful and happy life. In democratic Athens, success depended on the individual's ability to speak persuasively in the law courts and assemblies. So the Sophists used their powers of reason and understanding of human nature to develop public speaking into an art. They taught the means to gain audience approval as well as to present arguments clearly and logically. They practiced by arguing both sides of the question or concentrating their energies on the unpopular view. As philosophers, they developed balanced clauses and contrasting phrases to convey new and subtle ideas. As stylists, they groped for elaborate modes of expression which would make prose as dignified a vehicle for grand ideas as poetry had been.[4] Sometimes the results were ridiculous, but the power of the word had been unleashed, as Phaedra's protests to the all too persuasive nurse in Euripides' *Hippolytus* reveal.

> This is the deadly thing which devastates
> well-ordered cities and the homes of men—
> that's it, this art of oversubtle words.
> It's not the words ringing delight in the ear
> that one should speak, but those that have the
> power to save their hearer's honorable name.[5]

Both Strepsiades and Phidippides think they know all about the school next door, each from his own vantage point, but the inner sanctum exceeds their expectations. It contains a jumble of all the ideas and practices of the new philosophy, exaggerated and distorted and presided over by a comic caricature of "The Philosopher." The disciples train their reason and their senses on astronomy, cosmology, geometry, theology, and even climatology. According to the pupil who opens the door, Socrates has been engaged in the serious study of nature—measuring the jump of a flea and determining that a gnat buzzes through its bowels. Other pupils study things beneath the earth with their heads while their buttocks contemplate the heavens. Aristophanes gives the school a coherent cosmology which probably parodies the ideas of Diogenes of Apollonia, his contemporary.[6] Air is the primary substance from which everything else is generated through rarefaction and condensation. In eternal rotary motion like a whirlwind, air goes through many transformations in temperature and moisture, with heavy things forced into the center, lighter to the periphery. The comic chorus of Clouds presents a perfect symbol for this changeable, mobile, infinite first principle. It will be used, of course, to reflect the relativity of truth and morality as well. The metaphor for the cosmos itself is the charcoal burner's kiln, an oven shaped like an inverted bowl, holding charcoals surrounded by swirling flames and gases. Thus the esoteric scientific theory is reduced to a humdrum equivalent. Like the Sophists and Diogenes of Apollonia, Aristophanes' scholars view man as part of the natural continuum. In the comedy, all things, from the buzz of a gnat to thunder and lightning, can be explained in terms of the whirling movement of air in human bowels. The other aspect of the new philosophy, the art of rhetoric, is also trivialized by its comic presentation. Socrates tries to teach Strepsiades to speak effectively by emphasizing abstruse points of meter and gender. But Strepsiades refuses to learn what is so patently useless and ridicules Socrates' method by injecting a sexual connotation wherever he can.

The name of the school, the Thoughtery, is a loaded word. Coined from a combination of *phrontis* for thought and *telesterion*, the place of initiation into the mysteries, the name conveys the idea that philosophy itself is a religion which offers truth and life to its worshippers. The analogue is carried out in the opening scenes at the school. As early as line 113, the pupil refers to the events inside as mysteries. Strepsiades' admission parodies an initiation rite, complete with a sacred couch, a chaplet, powder for purification, a vision of the divine Clouds, and a naked entrance through a cavelike opening. The Clouds call on Socrates as the high priest.

Unlike the Eleusinian or Dionysiac mysteries, however, this new religion threatens to overthrow the Olympian gods. Antagonism to anthropomorphic myth was a feature of the new philosophy; Diogenes of Apollonia actually deified air. Here Socrates dismisses Strepsiades' antiquated ideas about religion with the line, "Zeus? What Zeus? Are you mad? There is no Zeus" (l. 367). He proceeds to prove that Zeus does not control natural phenomena or act according to human concepts of justice. It is really the Clouds, Aether, and the Whirlwind that produce the weather. But Socrates' new divinities seem unconcerned with moral questions. Convinced, Strepsiades uses this new knowledge against his unenlightened son and creditors.

The Socrates who directs the Thoughtery has always puzzled scholars. Aristophanes' presentation of him contrasts sharply with the martyr described by Socrates' younger contemporaries, Plato and Xenophon. Surely the historical truth lies somewhere in between. According to Plato's dialogues, Socrates studied natural philosophy as a young man, and was always eager to discuss moral and aesthetic questions with anyone, anytime, and anywhere. He never opened a school, however, and he never charged a fee to those who listened to him. But he was well known for his eccentricities. As he walked about the city, conversing with other philosophers, foreign and native, he was followed by troops of youths from prominent Athenian families. Fat and snub-nosed, he looked like a satyr, according to Alcibiades. Consciously ascetic, or so wrapped up in thought that he ignored physical discomfort, he went about barefoot and without a cloak, even in winter. Sometimes he lapsed into trances or conversed with strange spirits. Although the oracle at Delphi had called him the wisest of men, he spoke to all others as if they were his teachers. Thus he was the perfect subject on which to build the comic caricature of "The Philosopher" per se.

In 423 the fact that he had no school, refused money, believed devoutly in the gods, and was a staunch defender of moral absolutes was far less important than his notoriety. This comic transformation of the real Socrates is typical of the art form and can be paralleled in Aristophanes' distortion of other contemporaries. Socrates himself seems to have appreciated the joke.[7] In the early stages of the war when the state and its democratic system were still secure, neither the poet nor the philosopher could have foreseen that hostile citizens would confuse the two Socrates. Yet, in 399, after the defeat, because he was the old companion of two traitors, Alcibiades and Critias, he was blamed for the moral decline of the state. In Plato's *Apology,* Socrates complains that the comedy prejudiced his fellow citizens against him. The official charge reads like a summary of the character of the *Clouds.*

The Athenian citizen of 423 is as much a distortion as the philosopher is. Strepsiades is a typical comic hero, who acts as a buffoon to mock the pretensions of his opponent. Confronted with new ideas, Strepsiades vacillates between hyperbolic praise and earthy comments which disgust his guides. Both reactions underscore the triviality and uselessness of the pursuits in the Thoughtery and the ridiculous affectations of those who think themselves wise. Thus Strepsiades is actually practicing Socratic irony on the comic

Socrates. But his literal gut reaction to everything also exposes his own inability to transcend his preoccupation with himself and his immediate surroundings. While Socrates tries to teach him, Strepsiades can concentrate only on bedbugs. Sent to bed to think, he begins to masturbate instead. Thus, the confrontation of teacher and pupil provides a further antithesis. If Socrates is the effete intellectual who represents man's rational component, Strepsiades is the animal part, unable to apply his reason to anything beyond his body and instincts. Their humorous meeting demonstrates the incompleteness of each.

Strepsiades is no more moral than his teacher. He may represent positive values in opposition to his extravagant son but he schemes to satisfy his own needs by whatever means he can. When he is oppressed by debts, he rushes to the Thoughtery to learn to cheat his creditors. Nor does his faith in the traditional gods prevent him from error. The image of Zeus urinating through a sieve to cause rain is as preposterous as Socrates' explanation of the weather and is surely no standard by which to judge the new religion. The proof that lightning strikes Zeus' own sacred grounds destroys his belief in the Olympians as arbiters of a moral universe. He readily accepts the new divinities as soon as he realizes they can give him what he wants.

The chorus of Clouds is invoked by Socrates as part of Strepsiades' initiation ceremony. Their parodus is a magnificent religious lyric couched in the mythic language of the old religion. But these beautiful goddesses are the female divinities of the new religion, related to Aether, the Whirlwind, Chaos, and the Tongue. Socrates' description of their ability to transform their shapes provides an opportunity for lampooning individual thieves, perverts, and cowards in the audience. In addition, it emphasizes the role of the Clouds as metaphors for the physical and moral world of the play. Manifestations of the first principle of the cosmos, they are bags of air in eternal motion. They can also be seen as literal windbags, full of hot air, unsubstantial and meaningless like the pursuit of science and rhetoric. Or changeable and therefore subjective and relative, so the weaker argument can indeed appear the stronger. They have an immediate effect on Strepsiades; his soul is all in motion and he longs to quibble about hot air (l. 320). Now they promise to make him a successful speaker. Later, true to their ambiguous natures, they will reverse themselves completely and chastize him for his immoral desires.

After the Clouds have sent Socrates and Strepsiades into the school, they turn to address the audience. In the parabasis proper, the chorus leader speaks for Aristophanes to pray for the play's victory. He claims that the play was originally defeated because it was designed for the enlightened. Rather than depending on cheap tricks like extra-thick phalluses or violent beatings, he has always employed fresh themes with original characters and verses. Those who prefer his plays will be famous for their good judgment. It is interesting to note that he pitches his plea to the wise in the audience, separating them from the fools who understand only belly laughs. It is almost as if he is identifying himself, as the clever (*sophos*, l. 520) poet, with the Sophists in his drama. In fact he uses their techniques of persuasion and flattery to get the audience's approval and feed their own delusions of wisdom. He also connects Old Comedy itself, as practiced by his rivals, with the play's amoral world of chicanery and theft. Thus the satire recoils on the poet's art and the spectators who judge it.

For the rest of the parabasis, the chorus returns to its character as Clouds. The ode and antode are structured like a prayer of invocation.[8] They call upon the major Olympian gods, using familiar iconography and myth, but when they invoke their own father, Aether, as the universal sustainer of life, the conventional rhythm takes an unexpected turn. As in the parodus and the initiation scene, the old religion and the new cult are inexplicably fused. In the other parts of the lyric, the Clouds try to prove to the audience that they are really the gods; for they are the ones who protect the city. They also plead for another neglected goddess, the Moon, whose light saves money and who would straighten out their religious calendar if only they would respect her phases.[9] As the Clouds define themselves more closely in the parabasis, they seem more vague and ambiguous. Only names distinguish them and their associates from the older gods.

Socrates emerges from the Thoughtery swearing by Chaos, Air, and Respiration (a key term of Diogenes) because he is frustrated by Strepsiades' stupidity. Strepsiades, on the other hand, cannot learn what he considers useless. But Phidippides is young enough to apply his wits to the practical courses the Thoughtery offers. In the three-way scene which follows, the satire moves away from abstract philosophizing to the new pragmatism. The thievery of the teachers is suggested when Phidippides notices his father's cloak and sandals are missing. Socrates is very proud of the huge fee Hyperbolus has paid, and the Clouds advise him to fleece the father and son quickly. Socrates judges Phidippides too ignorant to plead a case and convinces him that he needs education to succeed in the world.

Socrates takes no part in the agon, the formal debate, between the Just and Unjust Discourses. Instead he withdraws to let Phidippides choose which curriculum he will study. The two emerge quarrelling and dressed in masks and feathers perhaps to look like fighting cocks.[10] As they shout insults and maxims at each other, several principles are established. The Unjust Discourse is certain that he can manipulate the audience because they are fools. The Just Discourse will rely on truth, assuming the audience wise enough to discern it. He, of course, believes that absolute truth and justice exist, established by the gods as standards by which man is judged and gains honor. Since the Unjust Discourse denies the existence of any such standard, he refuses to be insulted by assaults on his character. Instead, he turns his opponent's belief in Zeus against him by pointing out moral inconsistencies in Olympian mythology.

The two nearly come to blows before the chorus separates them and sets up the rules for a formal debate. The Just Discourse agrees to go first, encouraged by the Clouds and taunted by his rival's threats to destroy him with new ideas and subtle fancies. The Just Discourse presents a long well-reasoned argument to prove that his education produced modest prudent youths who were able to fully develop their minds and bodies and thus to live secure, happy, and honorable lives. In contrast, of course, to today's physically shrivelled moral degenerates who prefer the law courts to the gymnasia. Despite the rationality of his arguments, his examples belong to the comic world where "modest" is defined as covering up all traces of the genitals after sitting in sand and not daring to grab for meager meals of parsley before the elders have dined. The happy life becomes Elysium where garlanded youths delight in running races with virtuous friends and savoring the smells of trees.

They might as well be dead, the Unjust Discourse concludes, in his turn, for the older education deprives youth of all the pleasures of life—sex, drinking, and hearty laughter—and what is life worth without these? He has built up to this climax, not by a long speech, but by a series of short questions, compared to wrestling holds, whereby he is able to prove that tradition, represented by Homer and the gods, offers no precedent for this self-denial, or proof of benefits from it. Nor are there any dangers from giving in to pleasure, for the new education can teach you how to talk your way out of anything. When caught in the act by an irate husband, you can argue from Zeus' example; if even he was an adulterer, how can any weak mortal hope to restrain himself? The Unjust Discourse wins the contest when he gets the Just Discourse to admit that in truth everyone—advocates, poets, demagogues, in fact, all the spectators—is "broad-assed," that is, "has had a radish pushed up his anus to punish his adultery" (ll. 1083 ff.).

The debate demonstrates, in comic terms, the art of the new education and its effect on the younger generation. The techniques of rhetoric are skillfully revealed in both arguments.[11] The long speech of the Just Discourse can be divided into the sections suggested by contemporary handbooks. In both discourses, movements in the arguments are carefully separated by phrases such as "first of all" and "therefore," while commonplaces which emphasize "the just" and "the advantageous" appear everywhere. The Unjust Discourse demonstrates the relativity of truth by using myth for evidence. Behind the entire debate lies a theory of audience psychology and an assumption about the strength of man's natural drives. *Nomos,* with honor as its reward, represents the ideal for man. But, if everyone in the audience is a notorious adulterer, then *physis,* which acts from motives of self-interest, is the truth. The Sophists have shown the younger generation how to satisfy their *physis* painlessly by using clever speech to reduce *nomos* to antiquated propaganda. No wonder the youth flock to the courts and the courtesans, unconcerned by dishonor or damnation.

III   *Commencement: A Pyrrhic Victory*

Strepsiades hands his son over to the Unjust Discourse to be made a skillful Sophist, although the chorus, having extolled the virtues of the old wisdom, warns that the father may regret his decision. While Phidippides is being instructed, the chorus sings an ode promising rewards if the audience votes a first prize for *Clouds,* but threatening dire weather if it doesn't. Thus, the audience is tempted to judge according to fear and self-interest rather than by the abstract aesthetic standards discussed in the parabasis. Soon Strepsiades rushes out of his house, harassed by his debts and eager to cash in on his son's new skill. That Phidippides has acquired it is clear from his pallor and then from his magnificent proof of the inconsistencies in the legal definition of the due date of debts, constructed in part on the gluttonous nature of the magistrates who misuse it. Singing to the audience about how easily he will swindle them, Strepsiades leads his son in to a festive meal. Their party is interrupted, however, by creditors clamoring to be paid. Strepsiades demonstrates the success of his initial plan and the fool's clever use of useless wisdom as he drives them off. True to himself, however, he caps his own verbal quibbles by beating an injured creditor who is unable to fight back.

In an about-face, however, the chorus pronounces a moral judgment on Strepsiades, who is now at the height of his power. Because Phidippides has learned to use words to pervert justice, Strepsiades will wish that his son were dumb. The father now runs out on stage screaming for help because his son has been beating him. After the chorus calms the shouting match to establish orderly procedure, a second agon follows. Strepsiades recounts the events leading to the blows. Phidippides has responded to his simple request for an old song by Simonides or Aeschylus with one about incest by Euripides. Phidippides confidently offers to prove he was right to strike his father. And he does, destroying Strepsiades' arguments and proving the law man-made and capable of change. He also appeals to nature for precedents, showing how cocks fight with their fathers. Strepsiades finds the proper retort—"If you're a bird, go live on a perch"—but he is forced to concede that a son should beat his mother too. Now he realizes he was better off when his son whipped horses instead of him. At first, he blames the Clouds, but they plead the excuse of tragedy; they intentionally lead evil men to disgrace so they may learn to fear the gods. Now Strepsiades knows himself, and Zeus and Socrates as well. Although his son remains a zealous convert, the old man renounces his own impiety and sets the Thoughtery on fire. Turning Socrates' own words against him and his school into a real oven, he drives the inhabitants away, calling his act a punishment for blasphemy.

IV Ambiguities

Because the plot contains some inconsistencies, a few statements about the coherence of the comic vision of *Clouds* are necessary. In the first place, the play focuses on attempts of men to use their minds to comprehend and control their environment.[12] This attempt is ridiculed, first, by the suggestion that the philosopher concentrates on the trivial and utterly useless. Aristophanes accomplishes this by placing the boorish old man in the Thoughtery.

His exposure of the scholars' affectations shows how little of life's mysteries the human mind, trained or not, can actually grasp. But the attempt to be practical, to manipulate people and control events, is also doomed to failure. Phidippides' success at learning the Unjust Discourse demonstrates this. The son loses his virtue and his tan. Through him, Strepsiades gets what he wants, the power to cheat, but his victory is hollow, for he has created a monster who can outtalk him as well as his creditors. Socrates himself teaches too well. He loses the Thoughtery because of his star pupil.

Critics are sometimes puzzled by the fact that, although Phidippides has learned the Unjust Discourse, it is Strepsiades who drives the creditors away. But the playwright has used the two pupils to demonstrate the two different aspects of philosophy. As old man and fool, Strepsiades shows us the foolishness of the wise. Thus, he cannot be the one who learns his lessons easily on stage, and so Phidippides gets the pragmatic education. But Strepsiades is the comic hero, the one who conceives the plot to transcend the oppression in his life. Therefore, it is he who must demonstrate his success here by confidently outtalking the creditors. Although he falls from the heights of that glory to the depths of despair, beaten physically and verbally by his own son, he still gets the last word, or rather, blow. In a grand finale of self-assertion, of passion and instinct over intellect, he destroys his enemy. Thus he remains the triumphant hero, and the failure of his plan only emphasizes the entire play's exposure of man's pretensions to reason.

The ending has also created problems because the comic tone seems to disappear. The Clouds, the former patrons of Blasphemy and Deceit, suddenly announce that Strepsiades' plan is immoral and must fail. Strepsiades' comic heroism results in a beating instead of a victory, and his means to freedom, the Thoughtery, is burned down. Critics see evidence here of an unfinished revision more sympathetic to the old education and *nomos* than the version that was actually performed.[13] But it is a mistake to regard Strepsiades as a representative of the moral ideas expressed by the Just Discourse. He remains a comic hero: self-assertive, never restraining his will, preoccupied with his body, and, indeed, as much a cheat as the charlatan / philosopher. His reconversion at the end results only in the destruction of one more oppressor, the Thoughtery; it does not signify any change in character or means. Thus, the values defended in the Just Discourse are not embodied in any of the characters and represent only the comic opposition to the Unjust Discourse. The ending, then, simply disappoints Strep-siades' ambition without supporting an alternative.

The *Clouds* satirizes not only the new philosophy but philosophy itself, that is, man's love of wisdom and his faith in its power to comprehend, categorize, and control his life. Strepsiades at the beginning is a fool who thinks wisdom will help him get ahead. Socrates and his school represent a farrago of the various contem-porary attempts to explain life and the cosmos. Many antinomies are set up at the beginning—wise and foolish, old and new, city and country, rich and poor, *nomos* and *physis*, prudence and passion, Olympians and trinity of Clouds, Air and the Whirlwind. At first the distinctions are clear—thrifty father and extravagant son, ur-bane wife and rustic husband, pupil and teacher. But soon reversals and ambiguities begin to develop. The father goes to school in place of the son who then beats his father because parents are children twice over. The teacher is exposed by the fool as foolish and, despite his asceticism, self-centered. Once the Olympians are driven out, the new gods become suspiciously like the old. Although they begin by denying the *nomos* while using traditional music and myth, they end by taking over traditional morality as well.

The comic form itself underlines the blurring of distinctions by suddenly taking on the characteristics of tragedy.[14] The Clouds reveal that they have been instruments to lead a morally blind man to fear the gods, as if the entire action had been fated. Strepsiades himself accuses Socrates of sinful pride (*hybris*, l. 1506). Teachers and pupils lament with typically tragic groans when their respective nemeses strike. It is as if this spectacular parody has revealed the wisdom of the real Socrates to characters and audience. Having watched parent reduced to child, Clouds become Olympians, and comedy become tragedy, all must surely be aware they do not know what they think they know. As C. H. Whitman has pointed out, ". . . Aristophanes has shown singular skill in playing both ends of these antinomies, scarcely against the middle, but against each other, till both are attenuated and reduced to absurdity."[15] The Clouds are the grand poetic symbol of ambiguity, and their reversal emphasizes the folly of man's attempts to construct metaphysical systems and to label and control his world.

From the beginning, the members of the audience have been made part of the ambiguity. They are not only spectators of a com-edy but judges of the value of the play and the divinity of the Clouds. They have been manipulated by a chorus skilled in rhetoric to decide both on the basis of *nomos* (aesthetic standards) and *physis* (advantage to themselves). They are called alternately wise men and fools. Strepsiades even addresses them as food for the clever, sheep waiting to be fleeced (ll. 1201 ff.), thus picking up the animal metaphors of the parodus which make them part of the biological continuum. Any pretensions of morality are destroyed in the agon when they are all proved to be adulterers. The same spectators who probably laughed at the preposterous presentation of their religious beliefs might not have enjoyed seeing themselves dramatized as either corrupt or, worse, dupes of every clever speaker. But the poet includes himself in the satire. The final irony is that despite his pretensions to wisdom and to serious subject matter and his skill at persuasion, he too has failed. For he knows that the audience had once voted the play a third prize!

Within this framework, philosophy is defeated, but the comic hero is still triumphant, for the truth about man is that he must assert himself, must not deny his body, his passions, or his will. Phidippides, the younger version of his father, has lost his tan, but not the character natural to his youth. He is as fanatic a philosopher as he was an equestrian. And as rebellious a son, ever loyal to the opponent of his father, whether Uncle Megacles or Socrates. Nor is Strepsiades really defeated. He will not take his punishment like a tragic hero and accept the inevitable. He must do even the gods one better, and punish his enemy himself, fulfilling the demands of his will and passion while justifying his act to his victim and the audience. The shambles he makes of the Thoughtery is the dramatic depiction of the shambles that the comedy has made of the metaphysical structures man creates to control and oppress his true nature.

CHAPTER 4

Jurymen on Trial: Wasps (Sphēkes)

I *Summary*

IN 422 at the Lenaea, Aristophanes tried again. Like *Clouds*, *Wasps* is structured around an antithesis between the old and the new, represented by a father at odds with his son. And implicit in the resolution of the conflict is the same idea that human nature is irrepressible and impervious to educational reform. This time, however, Aristophanes chose instead of philosophy a target with a far wider appeal: the Athenian jury system, the keystone of the democracy, where the common man had absolute authority. (Perhaps the recent increase in pay to the jurors, initiated by the demagogue Cleon, influenced his choice of subject.) In addition, the comic hero of *Wasps*, unlike Strepsiades, is clearly triumphant over all his adversaries. Although his illusion of political power is stripped away, he replaces it with something better through his own resourcefulness. The drama culminates in a hilarious and bawdy combination of sex, insult, and song. Despite the poet's assertion that he should be prized for his political wisdom, Aristophanes has produced a play according to the accepted comic formula. Whether he was satisfied with the audience's verdict is uncertain; it seems *Wasps* came in second to *Proagon*, another play by Aristophanes

The plot of *Wasps* has a simple, coherent structure which emphasizes the comic movement from oppression to complete freedom. At the beginning the hero Philocleon (I love Cleon) is locked up by his son Bdelocleon (I hate Cleon) so that he cannot serve on the jury. All his valiant attempts to escape end in failure. When his fellow jurors, the Wasp Chorus, come to pick him up on their way to court, a battle ensues between them and his jailors. Bdelocleon offers to prove that the overzealous and arrogant jurors are in fact mere dupes of Cleon who work too hard for too little reward. He wins the agon easily, but the war is not yet over. First he must provide his court-starved father with a mock trial at home. But this ends in disaster because Philocleon finds the defendant innocent. Next he tries to change his father's life by introducing him to the tranquil pleasures of polite society. This too results in disaster for the son because the father refuses to fit the refined image of "aged parent" constructed for him. Instead, once free from the rigors of jury duty, the father finds a new younger self and ample opportunity for unrestricted pleasure. Philocleon's zeal leads not only to wild orgies, stolen women, and frenetic dancing, but, worst of all, it threatens to bring them both back to court, this time as defendants. Unconcerned, the father leads the actors and chorus off the stage, visibly overjoyed and oversexed.

II   *The Courts: Disease and Cure*

In the prologue, two slaves introduce the dramatic situation. While the master is asleep on the roof, his father is locked up inside, sick with a strange disease. Feigned guesses from the audience permit lampoons of individuals addicted to drinking, gambling, and sodomy. But the old man's addiction is even more perverse. His mania for jury duty and everything connected with the courts is destroying his sleep, his health, and his mind. All attempts to cure him having failed, the son is determined to keep him away from court by force. Though the house has been sealed up tight, the slaves have been posed as sentries, just in case, for the old man has been hopping around like a jackdaw, trying to get out. And they tell us the name of the pair, Philocleon, because he is addicted to Cleon, the current leader, and Bdelocleon, who has a "pompous snortical" nature.

Just then the action begins. Bdelocleon alerts the slaves to prevent his father's latest escape attempt. The old man's determination, animal cunning, and comic heroism are well established in this scene. Like a rat, he tries to get through the pipes, like smoke he climbs up the chimney, like a sparrow he pushes his way out the roof tiles. His words and insults are as clever as his schemes, and, true to the description of his mania, are usually associated with court procedure. A veritable Odysseus, he even plots to escape beneath a donkey being led to market and when caught, calls himself "Noman," parodying the famous Polyphemus episode of the *Odyssey*. But alas he is still an old man. Toothless, he cannot chew through the net placed around the house. He is reduced to calling on Cleon for help and throwing roof tiles down at the younger men who guard him.

But Bdelocleon knows the battle is not yet over. He is expecting his father's cronies to summon Philocleon to jury duty, as they do every morning before dawn. And he views them as worthy opponents, terrible as a swarm of wasps. The chorus of old men enters, led on by their sons. The scene, sung in part with the boys and Philocleon, who appears at an upper window, reveals their similarity to the comic hero. Old and feeble now, they are still courageous, refusing to be bullied by their sons and unafraid to tackle the younger opponents of their friend. And cunning too. They are full of clever suggestions for escape routes. They delight in recounting the old days when they were at the top of their form as valiant soldiers and crafty thieves. Their respect and love for Philocleon as the best of them all, then and now, makes them determined to defend him. Most important, they are suffering from the same disease—addiction to the courts and to Cleon. Eager to condemn, they suspect plots everywhere and conjecture that Philocleon's lateness is caused by his shock at yesterday's unprecedented acquittal. Moreover, they have already condemned Cleon's enemy, Laches, whose case is to come up today. Their mania is different from Philocleon's, however. Life in the courts gives him pleasure and a sense of importance. For them, it means survival itself; no court, no food, as the duet with their sons indicates. And the implication is that they get both their money and their instructions from Cleon.

At their urging, Philocleon gnaws through the net and tries to slide down from the second story. Caught in the act, he appeals for help to anyone in the audience who might need his vote in court this year. But it is the chorus who comes to the rescue. When they throw off their cumbersome cloaks, they reveal not phalluses but stiff sharp stings, the weapon by which they convict. They are full of fury and charges of treason, but they fall to the superior force of their opponents. Since Bdelocleon wants to persuade them that the court system does not benefit them, he offers to let them judge a debate between himself and his father. Meanwhile Philocleon has been reacting to the vicissitudes of battle with tragic laments and prayers in solemn rhythms. The parodies heighten the comic effect of his ludicrous requests (to be turned into a voting pebble) and his promises (not to fart or urinate on court statues). But the serious style also underlines his heroic, if comic, character, and the ultimate seriousness of the question. Like a tragic hero, he offers to fall on his sword, if defeated. For, if he is proved wrong, then old men will be good for nothing at all.

Philocleon agrees to accept his colleagues as jurymen and swears to abide by their verdict. With the chorus' encouragement, he begins the agon. In an arrogant and pseudoprofessional manner, Bdelocleon interrupts his father's speech occasionally to summarize or mark points for dispute. Philocleon argues that he gains great power and even greater pleasure from his work as a juryman. How like a king he feels when he is begged for mercy by rich thieves or when he permits defendants to indulge in transparent rhetorical tricks. Moreover, powerful demagogues pander to him while his family cherishes him as its breadwinner. In his excitement, he sees himself equal to the king of the gods, Zeus himself, as he hurls his thunder and lightning against the rich and the noble. The chorus join him in his ecstasy, imagining themselves divine judges over the dead, and rejoicing in his victory. But again they have prejudged the case. Bdelocleon recognizes the difficulty of healing their disease, long endemic to Athens and too important for comedy (ll. 650 - 51), but he undertakes to cure it. With graphic examples, he proves they are kept in line and overworked for very little money while their so-called protector gets the lion's share of the huge revenues of the empire. The chorus concedes and urges their friend to be grateful for his son's love and concern.

But Philocleon is too much an individual to give up his means of self-definition easily. His sense of loss is overwhelming. His hand is so numb he cannot draw his sword. Nor does he speak at once. Suddenly he bursts into a tragic lament, refusing comfort and demanding to be taken to court, this time to convict Cleon for theft. His full cure will require further treatment; he will be allowed to conduct mock trials at home and to decide domestic disputes amidst all the comforts. A parody of the solemn rites of law ensues when Philocleon impatiently demands all the objects and ceremonies of the real court. Bdelocleon obliges, serving his physical needs as well; the chamber pot doubles as a waterclock used for timing speeches. After the opening invocations, Bdelocleon presents the case of the dog Labes charged by another dog with stealing the Sicilian cheese. Since the defendant can only bark, Bdelocleon pleads for him, using all the stock devices of oratory. Philocleon has of course judged Labes guilty before hearing the case, but he is distracted by the need to urinate, the temptation of lentil soup, and his own tears over the squealing puppies of the thief. Bdelocleon leads him to the voting urns and tricks him into putting his pebble into the wrong one. Once the old man discovers he has voted for acquittal, his mania is destroyed. Full of self-reproach at his weakness, he allows his son to take over his life.

The Athenian jury system is put on trial in the agon and domestic tribunal. Of course, here as elsewhere, the comedian distorts and exaggerates to make the audience laugh. Much of the humor derives from the presentation of the familiar in a ludicrous way. The audience would immediately recognize the parody of legal procedure, the profane treatment of sacred court objects and rituals, and the exposure of rhetorical tricks. Probably most of the spectators had been in court themselves, as jurors or defendants. For one of the outstanding characteristics of democratic Athens was its litigiousness. The number of extant orations and rhetorical handbooks, as well as the ubiquitous threats of suits in comedy, testify to this. Moreover, the fear of lawsuits indicates that, although judgment by one's peers is a keystone of democracy, the court system could appear to the inexperienced individual as a means of oppression. Thus the mockery of its solemnity helps dispel the awe and anxiety citizens might feel about this arm of the government.

Athens was the legal center of the empire. Almost all cases, civil and criminal, local and international, were tried in the city with Athenian citizens as jurors, called diecasts.[1] At first, they probably served without pay, but around 462 Pericles established a small honorarium. By 424 Cleon had raised the salary to three obols a day, enough to buy a cheap meal, according to the chorus, or to clean a cloak, according to Philocleon. Each year six thousand jurors were chosen from a list of volunteers over age thirty, but without any other special qualifications. They were then divided into panels of five hundred or more as the trials came up. (The huge size of the panels was considered a safeguard against bribery or coercion of individual members.) The speeches of the plaintiff and defendant were the most important part of the trial. Because there was no rule which limited the speaker to statements that he could prove with evidence, each party was free to introduce almost any argument to persuade the jury. In the trial, the magistrates functioned to insure orderly procedure; they had no judicial powers of their own. After hearing both sides, the individual jurors voted for or against the defendant, and the verdict of the majority was not subject to appeal. Small wonder that the Athenian populace could view the legal system as proof of its supremacy.

But Aristophanes' satire of the jurymen-wasps presents some serious criticism of the way the system works in practice.[2] Because the younger able-bodied men were away at war or struggling to make a living of more than three obols, the jurors tended to be all old men who viewed the function as a permanent job or kind of old-age pension. They were thus bound to the demagogue who could insure their salary. The chorus suggests that Cleon has instructed them to vote in the upcoming trial against Laches. They derive more than money from their jury duty, however. Once valiant warriors who drove away the barbarians, they are now feeble old men living on memories. Both Philocleon and the chorus boast that jury duty makes them feel like men again, or even gods, when like Zeus they weigh the fates of defendants. And they feel most godlike when they use their power to condemn. So they are always hunting for traitors, always ready to vote guilty before the evidence is in. Their long sharp stings symbolize the stylus used to draw the long line indicating the maximum sentence. Aristophanes implies, through the humorous treatment of their mania, that they have perverted justice because of their economic and psychological needs.

The poet's picture of the wasps is ultimately sympathetic; they are described as dupes of the demagogues. However, Aristophanes accuses the politicians of more than bribery of the jury. The Athenian practice of examining the records of public officials after their terms of office had expired often led to charges of peculation or misconduct. Scholars suggest that Cleon was a legal witchhunter who made a practice of prosecuting his political enemies to enrich the public treasury and himself.[3] Instigated by Cleon, the wasps all rush to the trial of Laches, a general charged with peculation in Sicily. Whether there ever was such a trial is conjectural. The real Laches did lose a battle in Sicily in 427, but since he fought again at Delium in 424 and had just negotiated a truce in 423 he must not have been convicted of any crime. He would be a natural enemy of Cleon's, however, since he was an oligarch and had just made peace.

The mock trial of the dogs is a transparent allegory of what the court proceeding might have been.[4] The dog's name, Labes, means "Grab" and is an obvious pun on Laches, whereas the plaintiff is called Cuon ("Dog"), which sounds like Cleon. Both animals come from the same district as the politicians they represent, and the stolen cheese is Sicilian. Cuon accuses Labes of the same offenses

charged against Cleon in the agon. Bdeloeleon's defense of Labes
satirizes the way in which pleaders demean both themselves and the
jurors to win their cases. He resorts to irrelevant praise, lame excuses, counteraccusations, and the testimony of a witness who is
probably implicated in the crime (the cheese-grater/paymaster may
represent Laches' treasurer). He concludes his defense with an
attempt to arouse the judge's pity; the starving whimpering puppies
of Labes come forward to beg for their father's acquittal. Philocleon
has decided beforehand that Labes is guilty, but one look at Cuon
assures him the plaintiff is another Labes. The vote for acquittal is a
trick. Both dog-politicians are guilty in both men's eyes. But the
audience must judge the system guilty as well, for it depends upon
the persuasion of jurors who are unable to make impersonal
decisions based on points of law.

The satire of the jury system ends when Philocleon agrees to let
his son reform his life. The parabasis which follows employs the imagery of the interrupted drama to reproach the audience for not ap-
preciating the talent and courage of the poet. His heroic attack on
the Cleon monster who preys upon the citizens parallels
Bdeloeleon's attack on the demogague to save his father. The
description of Cleon as a mythical combination of beasts un-
derscores his essentially animal nature and associates him with the
wasps, Philocleon, and the lampooned spectators. Like Bdeloeleon,
the poet has also tried to purify the city of the chills and fever that
pile up lawsuits for the unwary—a clear reference to disease and
litigiousness. The identification of the altruistic poet with the
youthful reformer suggests that the citizen-spectators, like
Philocleon and the wasps, need reforming. The audience's failure to
select the best comedy clearly resembles the jurors' inability to
judge wisely and impartially. Thus, the parabasis almost makes the
playwright and his audience characters in the drama whose attitudes and actions must be tested with the actors in the following
scenes.

III   *The New Man*

In the ode and antode of the parabasis, the members of the
chorus again become Wasps, singing of the contrast between their
former vigor and their present weakness. The other parts of the lyric
explain the wasp metaphor in detail. They resemble the flying
beasts in their stings, waspwaists, and irrascible natures as well as in

their social habits. Although their physical prowess is gone, they prefer their waspish old age to the moral weakness of the younger generation. Moreover, it is clear that the old men are justly proud of their accomplishments. The subtle increase in sympathy toward them here prepares for the change which occurs in the following scenes when Bdelocleon's illusions of reform are destroyed by man's waspish nature.

Philocleon comes out of his house protesting loudly because his son wants to throw away his beloved old cloak. In the scene that follows, we are presented with the familiar confrontation between the fool and the quack. Philocleon's candid reaction to his son's attempts to turn him into a sophisticate reveals the affectations of the young reformer. The imported clothes he considers chic are, in fact, more expensive and more uncomfortable than their Athenian versions. The most fashionable sandals he recommends are actually made by the enemy, and Philocleon refuses to put them on because one of his big toes is a Sparta-hater. Father and son progress from clothes to deportment—how to strut, how to recline gracefully, how to impress your listeners with clever conversation. Like clothes, the latest manners are effeminate, constraining, and phony. When Bdelocleon suggest telling stories of gentlemanly experiences in an elegant manner, Philocleon responds bluntly with a story about his stealing a vine pole and defeating a famous racer in court. Bdelocleon then tests his father's ability to sing *skolia*, the drinking songs where one must link his verses to those of the previous singer. Philocleon adds not what the singer might expect, but what he really thinks and feels—that is, honest advice, insults, and accusations. As they prepare for the old man's debut at a drinking party, Philocleon naively warns his son against getting drunk and fighting, which will get him arrested and fined. Not in polite society, Bdelocleon assures him. If you apologize with literary allusions and graceful jokes, the injured party will overlook the incident. Philocleon takes this remark as an open invitation; "I'll learn lots of stories then, if I can get off, whatever wrong I do (ll. 1262 - 63)."

While they are gone, the chorus performs a second parabasis.[5] Again their address to the audience refers indirectly to the dramatic situation. First they lampoon two old men, one for giving up his pleasures and the other for taking pride in sons who are in fact effeminate perverts. Thus the sarcasm is a comment on the preceding episode. It is no longer clear who needs reform or who can provide it. Nor is any public principle more important than private pleasure. The poet's defense of moderating his attack on Cleon proves the point. He has discovered he has been fighting alone, for the citizens he wants to save only watch to derive pleasure from the poet's humiliation. In the scene which follows, Bdelocleon too will concede defeat to the pleasure principle.

But while the chorus has been speaking, Bdelocleon's party has degenerated into a drunken brawl. Philocleon's slave, Xanthias, enters, nursing his wounds, and regretting that he did not have a tortoise's shell to protect him. He describes Philocleon's antics: "he leapt, he skipped, he laughed and whinnied like an ass," insulting well-known guests and mugging passersby on his way home. The drunk enters now, dragging a nude flute girl and sporting a giant erection. When his son tries to return the abducted girl to her angry owner, the old man pretends she's a torch, lewdly explaining away its curiously feminine features. With educated allusions and good-humored jokes, he brushes off the threats of other pursuers, but they react with outrage.

As Bdelocleon pulls him inside for protection, his cronies sing a song of envy which emphasizes the comic reversal.[6] How lucky their friend is to have replaced the austere existence of a juryman with the easy life. And how lucky to have a son who is willing to indulge it. For although Bdelocleon is not happy about the results, he offers to pay damages and he resigns himself to a new mania. From drinking and sex Philocleon turns to directing a wild dance contest which pits the old steps against perverted modern ones. Bdelocleon and Xanthias stare in amazement from the side lines as the frenzied dancing begins. Literally ecstatic, Philocleon usurps the role of the leader and ushers the surprised chorus out of the orchestra to end the play.

IV   The Triumph of Hedonism

Many scholars have criticized the final scenes of *Wasps* because the satire against the jury system is dropped after the trial. They believe that Aristophanes included the rest only to satisfy the people's demands for farce, slapstick, and obscenity.[7] But its very vulgar form is absolutely necessary to dramatize the triumph of the life-force in nature which Old Comedy celebrates. The political satire is only a part, not the whole. Demagogues and the abuses of the legal system represent the social forces which restrain the individual. The comic hero must also confront the physical and cosmic oppression he feels. The approach of death, which all men fear and repress, is symbolized by the ubiquitous nostalgia for youth and the antagonism between father and son or old and new. When Philocleon demolishes his son's belief in reform and refinement with his fool's wisdom and then with his fists, he proves that nothing is really new and the old way is always best. This is underlined by the chorus' lampoons and the frenzied dance contest. But this cannot be assigned to the conservatism of the poet; rather it arises from the wish-fulfillment inherent in comedy. For in the comic fantasy, the hero not only defeats the new, but becomes young again himself. The toothless old man begins his rise by gnawing the net and ascends to full potency, able to outtalk, outfight, and outsex everybody. He takes over everything, even the functions of the chorus. He even tells the flute girl he's the son who won't inherit until his guardian Bdelocleon is dead (ll. 1352 - 55). He is more than rejuvenated, however. As a juror, he imagined himself a king and a god, but by the end of the play Xanthias recognizes his supernatural powers and calls him a *daemon* (l. 1475), capable of defeating death itself.

His triumph expresses man's freedom to assert his individuality and to seek satisfaction without restraint. Philocleon thinks that as a juror he is doing just that and demonstrates the force of his wit and his will. But this method of self-assertion is mere delusion. Once the jury madness is cured, Philocleon embraces hedonism, unafraid or unconscious of law, other people, or his own physical limitations. Throughout the play he is described in animal imagery which emphasizes the supremacy of the survival instinct over all types of restraint. He is a jackdaw and a rat at the beginning, but at the end he dances the steps of Phrynicus like a cock. Moreover, almost everyone in the play, from Cleon to the sons of Carcinus/Crab, to the audience itself, is described in terms of this imagery, often with witty reference to Aesop's fables. *Wasps* seems to offer this parallel as the comic truth about human nature: that we are all animals operating according to our own interests, always motivated by our instincts and acting with animal cunning, despite our pretensions to higher ideals. Does this then make Aristophanes anti-intellectual? More likely, the comedian is emphasizing this side to celebrate man's relation to the dynamic, amoral, and eternal life of nature.

The other side—the attempt to be reasonable, to reform ourselves, or to control our instincts—is soundly defeated. This theme is developed throughout in the disease / cure image. The susceptibility of both Philocleon and the spectators is established early in the prologue. His jury madness is finally healed, only to be replaced by a new frenzy. During the frenetic dance scene, Xanthias calls for hellebore to cure the latest mania (l. 1489), but it is clear that he and his master no longer believe they can stop the old man from being himself. In the two parabases, the poet associates himself with the reformers who would cure society's madness. Like Heracles, he has attempted to fight the monsters who threaten his people. But he turns the joke against himself too, for he recognizes that the audience is interested only if they get pleasure from the fight. Even if the audience does not delude itself about its social conscience, it takes as much pride in its cultural refinement and sophistication as the poet does. But the joke is on the spectators too. Bdelocleon, that humorless idealist, thinks that the latest in elegant dress and witty conversation is a sure sign of self-control. The brawl and the fury of the people who pursue Philocleon, however, demolish these delusions.

Despite the apparent futility of man's impulse toward reform, we are not left with a pessimistic vision. The ridicule of the important business of poets, parents, and citizens provides a sacred release. Man justifiably takes himself and his institutions seriously. And indeed the achievements of fifth-century Athens indicate what idealism and human reason can accomplish. But the comic vision purges man of the suspicion that, despite concepts like justice and honor, we love ourselves and our pleasures best, or that, despite effort, talent, and will, life is all "sound and fury, signifying nothing." Comedy temporarily transports the spectator to a world where nothing matters but pleasure, and man is free, for the moment at least, of all fear of failure because terms like success and failure have been rendered meaningless.

CHAPTER 5

Dirty Politics: Knights (Hippēs) and Birds (Ornithes)

I Knights

POLITICS was everybody's business in Aristophanes' Athens. The citizens chose their magistrates annually, took part in all major policy decisions, and then held each official legally responsible for his record. Thus the democratic system itself was an obvious target for Old Comedy's satire. And the two indispensible elements of the system, the demos, or sovereign people, and its leaders, the demagogues, received their share of the abuse. Aristophanes first approached the subject in *Babylonians*, a lost play, in which he at-' tacked the foreign policy of the demagogue, Cleon. According to *Acharnians* (l. 377), Cleon responded with a suit for lese majesty, but we have no evidence of what really happened.[1]

Two years later, Aristophanes attacked Cleon again in *Knights*. The Peloponnesian War was still going on, but it had taken a new turn in 424. The Athenians were blockading a Spartan force near Pylos on the Peloponnese, and the frightened Spartans were offering huge concessions. Cleon, however, persuaded the Athenians to hold out for total surrender. When he boasted that he could defeat them quickly, General Nicias called his bluff and resigned his command in Cleon's favor. The lucky demagogue reached Pylos just as General Demosthenes achieved a decisive victory. He returned home as the conquering hero and was elected general himself the following year.

This incident provides the starting point for *Knights*, a bitter satire on politics and politicians. The play is built around a central allegory.[2] One household represents the Athenian state. Its master, Demos, from the political district of Pnyx, stands for the Athenian demos, the sovereign people who controlled the assembly that met on the hill of the Pnyx. Described by his slaves as an old, bad-

71

tempered, bean-loving boor, Demos is both a private individual and a political group. Those beans that are his favorite food were the ballots of the assembly as well as the national dish. His old slaves, servants of household and state, are unnamed in the manuscripts, but allusions to the Pylos incident (ll. 55 ff.) indicate that they are the two generals, Nicias and Demosthenes.[3]

When the play begins, these two are bewailing the turn of events; a new slave, a Paphlagonian tanner has taken control of the household. He steals credit for the work done by other slaves, spies on them, charges protection, and has them beaten into silence. By lies, bribes, oracles, and flattery, he has turned the household upside down; Demos, the master, trusts only this slave and is completely ruled by him.[4] The term Paphlagonian defines the tanner as both a servile foreigner and a "Blusterer" (from the verb *paphladzo*). His trade associates him with the low commercial class of peddlers and craftsmen.[5] He is never referred to by name, and he wears no portrait mask because, as Demosthenes explains, no maskmaker has the courage to fashion his likeness (l. 231). Demosthenes assures the audience, however, that they are clever enough to recognize him. And, indeed, from the topical allusions, it is clear that the Paphlagonian is Aristophanes' old enemy, Cleon.

The play dramatizes the means by which Demos is pried away from Cleon's disastrous influence by a sausage seller, Agoracritus, a servant even more vulgar and deceitful than Cleon himself. With the encouragement of Nicias and Demosthenes, and the support of the Knights, the Athenian cavalry class, the sausage seller defeats the Paphlagonian in a series of contests in which topical allusions abound and familiar political sins are cloaked in the imagery of the combatants' coarse and violent trades. The processes of stuffing, gourmandizing, and digesting sausages are developed into a major metaphor for the voracious appetite and disgusting habits of the demagogue. But the metaphor reflects on Demos as well, for, with a different accent, his name means "fat" instead of "people."

The first contest is a shouting match before the Knights and Demos' slaves. In the next contest, the two men address the Athenian Council. Agoracritus tops Cleon's ultimate offer of peace with an announcement of a sale on anchovies which breaks up the meeting. The final contest is a long formal agon in which Demos himself sits as judge at the Pnyx and chooses between the rivals who offer themselves as his lovers. Like the household allegory, this analogy is also topsy-turvy, for the old man behaves like a young boy and is easily seduced by the sausage seller's gifts of expensive clothes and food. But the tanner refuses to give up until Demos has heard his oracles because he is certain that he is destined to offer a more glorious fortune to him. As both read and interpret their collections, they parody the enigmatic style and self-serving practices of wily oracle mongers. They also feed Demos' fantasy of being master not only of the household but of the world. The sausage seller wins again, this time by promising near-immortality. Cleon accepts final defeat only when he discovers that the sausage seller is the very rogue destined to defeat him.

Once the Paphlagonian has been silenced, the sausage seller uses his new position and special skills to cook Demos down to the essence of a proper master and to set the household and state right-side-up again. Demos is transformed into the sole ruler of Hellas, dressed in the simple dignified costume of the citizens of old. He is able to admit his former faults and demonstrate his new awareness of his responsibilities. Demos' rejection of his former suitors and their seductions also sets the love metaphor straight. The sausage seller presents him with a beautiful dancing girl, Treaty, an epiphany of the thirty-year peace the Paphlagonian has been hiding. His rebirth into a proper leader of his household and state is dramatized by his enthusiastic reaction to her as a woman and as a political personification of peace.

The ending of the play has been condemned by critics because it seems so illogical and unexpected. The household allegory gives way to the purely political. The sausage seller who has triumphed only because he is a worse soundrel than Cleon turns out to be a great reformer. And Demos, who has proved himself as voracious as his demagogues, is completely transformed into the noble ruler of Athens' good old days.

But there are several points to be noted in response to this criticism. In the first place, Demos has outgrown the household allegory in the course of the contests. Fed and flattered by both the tanner and the sausage seller, he is no longer content to be master of his household. As they recite their oracles, he dreams of becoming a tyrant or the great king of Persia, under the special protection of Athena.

It is true that the sausage seller is a degenerate, superior to the tanner only in flattery, bribery, and lying. The sausage seller has another side, however. He appears mysteriously, "as if by divine will" (l. 147), as soon as Nicias and Demosthenes discover that the oracles predict Cleon's defeat by a sausage seller. His allies refer to him as "having superhuman skill" (l. 141), term him "Blessed" in line 148, and three times call him "Savior" (ll. 149, 199, and 458). By the end, even Cleon recognizes Apollo's direction behind the events of the contests (l. 1240). This agent of the gods triumphs through baseness for two reasons. An innocent moralist would not stand a chance against the wiles of Cleon. Moreover, Demos himself is incapable of selecting a responsible leader / servant; he is only interested in feeding his own needs. When he chooses the sausage seller as steward, Demos reveals the depths of his own degeneracy. But when he recognizes that the sausage seller has indeed been divinely sent, his transformation begins.

Agoracritus effects a drastic reversal of a political and personal situation. His association with Apollo and oracles has led several critics to conclude that Aristophanes was imitating the structure and themes of Sophocles' *Oedipus Rex* in which King Oedipus rules Thebes without knowing that he has murdered his father, who was the former king, and is now married to his own mother, the past and present queen of Thebes. The relationship between the two plays helps to explain the radical ending in *Knights* as well as to indicate a date for the production of the tragedy.[6] There are several verbal coincidences in the plays, but the most striking similarity is that the ruler of the household and state is in a false position and does not know who he is or the consequences of his rule. In *Oedipus Rex*, the plague sets the search for truth in motion, whereas the sausage seller performs the same function in *Knights*. His challenge to Cleon forces the issue to a head. In both plays the oracles of Apollo are a central factor; Cleon and Oedipus, in trying to prove them false, both end by vindicating them. Cleon's excited questions to the sausage seller, particularly about his birth and youth, parody Oedipus' questions to the messenger and the herdsman and lead to a real tragic recognition and reversal. Before their moments of truth both Oedipus and Demos have revealed the extent of their pride (*hybris*) and sense of self-sufficiency. Oedipus hopes that he may be a son of the gods whereas Demos boasts that he is a ruler in full control who profits by his cleverness. Agoracritus is revealed as the child of destiny, and Cleon laments his fall in tragic style. The final scenes exhibit a further resemblance. Oedipus appears in his fallen state, blind and weak, to declare his new self-knowledge and self-acceptance and to restore order in the Theban state and in his family. Demos, his comic double, similarly emerges in his risen state, rejuvenated, clearly "knowing himself," and finally able to lead Athens and his household responsibly.

The play seems to be a rather bitter indictment of motivations and policies of both the sovereign people and the leaders they elect. The citizen body is, of course, satirized for its selfishness, stupidity, and self-delusion. It is easily led and rejects those who have served well in their time. Demos is the most obvious target in the play, but he is not the only one. The members of the council also sell out—for anchovies—and in the parabasis the audience is accused of the same faults because it has abandoned its favorite poets to shame and poverty in old age when their ideas are no longer fashionable. Using the imagery already associated with Demos and the demagogues, the chorus suggests that the spectators are also foolish, fickle, voracious men who callously devour and discard their servants, whether entertainers or politicians.

The Paphlagonian tanner corresponds in some respect to the historical Cleon. He was the son of a wealthy leather merchant, a very persuasive speaker, an active leader in the assembly, and a general who acted to prevent peace, according to Thucydides. He may have sued Aristophanes or his producer Callistratus for their criticisms of his harshness to the allies. As Dover has shown, translation of the real man into the comic slave of Demos owes much to the language of political backbiting.[7] His epithet "Paphlagonian," which denotes bombast, also suggests that his citizenship and thus his credentials for leadership are suspect. Instead of a wealthy manufacturer, he becomes a foreign-born tanner—a cheap, coarse trader. Both insults are typical attacks against political opponents. His pretensions to be lover and watchdog of the state also come from stock phrases of political oratory. Thus, it seems that the Paphlagonian tanner represents not only the current popular leader but all leaders whose tactics and pretensions never change. The *Knights* won first prize, but Cleon was elected general shortly after the Lenaea.

II *Summary of* Birds

In 414 Aristophanes presented *Birds* at the Great Dionysia under the name of Callistratus. Although the play won only a second prize, it is very popular with modern audiences because of its plot and lyricism as well as its spectacle. To readers familiar with earlier plays of Aristophanes, the social satire in *Birds* appears to lack a focal point. There is no hostility to war, as in *Acharnians* and *Peace*, no extended lampoon like those of Cleon and Socrates, nor is there any one institution, whether the schoolhouse, the courts, or the assembly, which bears the brunt of the criticism. Yet, the spring of 414 would seem to have been a time full of possibility for trenchant satire. That grand armada, the Sicilian expedition, had sailed away the summer before, with the almost unanimous approval of the citizens, carrying the men, resources, and hopes of the empire west toward a grandiose expansion of power. This action, however, negated the Peace of Nicias, and Nicias himself, later chosen co-leader of the expedition, disapproved of the scheme. The other leader, Alcibiades, had been implicated in the desecration of the Herms (religious images) before sailing and, summoned back that winter to face charges of impiety, had just deserted to Sparta. The expedition seemed foredoomed not only by the sacrilege but also by the political strife which prompted the recall of Alcibiades and by the defection of the brilliant general. But the only specific reference to these events occurs at line 148 when an actor expresses fear of the Salaminia, a public ship that had been sent to Sicily for Alcibiades. Thus it has been suggested that Aristophanes, either afraid to attack so important an undertaking or sensitive to national anxiety, avoided politics and created a witty and spectacular but essentially escapist fantasy.[8]

As Dover points out, however, there is no reason to assume that Aristophanes, at the time of writing, or the audience at the performance had any foreboding about the expedition.[9] None of the events that precipitated the disaster of 413—Sicily's unified defense, Sparta's aid to Syracuse, Nicias' tactical errors, the permanent Spartan occupation in Attica—could be foreseen in 414 when the army had just moved out of its winter quarters to begin the attack.

Birds is anything but apolitical; its target, however, is the national spirit responsible for the conception and execution of the expedition. The play is probably not a specific political allegory, with the hero representing Alcibiades, the birds the Athenians or the allies, and the gods the Spartans. The symbolism is too cryptic to suggest such exact correspondence.[10] It is certainly, however, a satire of political life in general, with the hero as the persuasive egotistical demagogue whose imagination and sheer bravado always win, the birds as the fickle mob who rush zealously from craze to craze and allow themselves to be victimized, and the gods as the pompous enemy who can be manipulated because they are just plain folks with the same bellies and buttocks as the rest of us.[11] The play's grandiose scheme, the fast-breaking events, the swarms of individuals who rush in to get their share, in fact the persistent motion toward the goal, all dramatize the unique spirit of the Athenian state. The national characteristic, termed *polupragmosune*, a key word in the play, provides the central theme and satiric target of *Birds*. As William Arrowsmith has pointed out, in the introduction to his translation: "On the positive side it connotes energy, enterprise, daring, ingenuity, originality and curiosity; negatively it means restless instability, discontent with one's lot, persistent and pointless busyness, meddling interference, and mischievous love of novelty. . . . In political terms, *polupragmosune* is the very spirit of Athenian imperialism, its remorseless need to expand, the *hybris* of power and energy in a spirited people. . . "[12]

The plot of the play moves ahead steadily from plan to resolution without the formal interruptions and premature solution more traditional in Old Comedy. It begins when two citizens, Pisthetaerus ("Friend of the Plausible") and Euelpides ("Son of Good Hope"), harassed by the complexities of urban life, abandon Athens in search of a simpler society. Taking the curse "Go to the birds" or "Go to Hell" literally, they wander off, each with a bird in hand, to seek advice from Hoopoe, once an Athenian hero but now transformed into a bird. After Hoopoe describes the birds' pastoral existence, Pisthetaerus is so enthused he conceives a grand idea—to help the birds found a city in the sky and establish an empire by overthrowing the Olympians. He persuades Hoopoe that his scheme is both plausible and advantageous, but the tribes of birds, once summoned to vote in the parodus, are less easy to convince. They view man as their natural enemy, who traps them in painful devices, hangs them in market stalls, and cooks them in disgusting sauces. The humans barricade themselves and suffer a ferocious attack with beaks and wings before Hoopoe calms the hostile birds. A truncated agon follows in which Pisthetaerus first proves the birds' inherent right to rule and then shows them a means to regain their lost realm.

While Hoopoe leads the men inside to get their wings, the bird chorus sings the parabasis, accompanied by Procne, the nightingale, Hoopoe's wife. The birds remain in character throughout all the parts of their address to the audience, enumerating their services so that the audience will elect them gods, and presenting a cosmology which proves their precedence. They end the parabasis by inviting all men to join their city, elaborately comparing human types to bird species. Once the actors emerge, the two-pronged aggression begins. The city is built and fortified, despite interruptions by ambitious mortals, and then thrown open to humans eager to become bird-men. Meanwhile the gods are brought to terms, first by the interception and near rape of Iris on her way to earth, and next, with the help of Prometheus, by the capitulation of an embassy of starving divinities. The play ends with the wedding of Pisthetaerus to Basileia, the royal princess who supervises the social, political, and military organization of Olympus for Zeus.

III   Democracy—For the Birds?

The prologue of the play presents a stark contrast to the national spirit described earlier. Two characters wander about a rocky pathless thicket with no sign of civilization. Several important themes and images are introduced as the humans explain themselves. In the first place, they are comic heroes, not model citizens. They are fleeing the city because it limits their freedom to do as they please. To them the ideal life consists of having the leisure and freedom to sponge off others and seduce the sons of their friends. Although unwilling to honor their debts, they do not want to suffer the legal consequences of welshing on them. They are citizens nonetheless, patriotic, and proud of their families. They cannot even conceive of life outside a city (l. 47), and as soon as they discover that the birds have ample food and no debts, they want to found one for them. But their ideal is a political community purged of all foreigners and all obligations. Hoopoe suggests more than he realizes when he asks if the two are looking for an aristocracy. Although they recoil in horror at his question, the city they construct differs from Athens only in that they become the rulers instead of the ruled.

The metaphorical relation between man and bird is also established early in the play. The Athenians are compared unfavorably to crickets; the latter chirp on their boughs only two months a year whereas the Athenians sing in the courts for their entire lives. The men have "flown away on both feet" (l. 35) from society, turning the saying "to the crows" into a reality. The frightened humans, covered with their own feces, introduce themselves to the slave-bird of Hoopoe with names that are scatological puns on species of birds and suggest their common physiological functions. The birds, however, have their own negative qualities, summed up in our cliché "birdbrain." But the birds have something men want—the ability to fly, which represents freedom and the knowledge of the mysteries of life.

At this point the relation is only a metaphor, for the two humans lack wings and are stuck on the ground. But an ideal combination of man and bird is presented in the character borrowed from tragedy, Tereus the hero metamorphosed into a hoopoe by Sophocles. He possesses the fortuitous combination of bird prowess and human ingenuity. He has convinced his slave to also become a bird in order to serve him. Bearing the human's burden with responsibility, he has made himself leader of the mob of birds, and although he judges his charges dullwitted and undignified, he has taught them to speak Greek. But Tereus / Hoopoe is a mythical king and an Athenian by marriage only. He is incapble of conceiving the outrageous scheme hit upon by the citizen of the democracy. He does understand its implications, however, and uses all his skill to manipulate his forces into approving the plan. After his success, he gives the humans their wings and disappears. Pisthetaerus, the selfish common man of Athens, becomes the real bird-man, who refuses to restrain his brash cunning, physical power, and ambition.

With the help of the nightingale, Hoopoe summons the birds to hear the scheme of Pisthetaerus. His words, punctuated with bird calls such as tio tio tio tinx, emphasize the beauty of their songs, their power to fly anywhere, and their freedom to devour the rich produce of nature. The audience must have witnessed a veritable "sound and sight" show as the birds entered the orchestra in brilliant costumes reciting elaborate lyrics. Twenty-eight different species are named.[13] As the first few enter one by one, comments on their plumage and mannerisms satirize human individuals and bird types. The Callias is the bird without feathers, so honest the informers have plucked him clean. The parodus song turns sour, however, when the birds discover Hoopoe has been harboring a human. Screeching treachery, they form into squadrons and attack with their beaks at the command of their leader. Hoopoe, the voice of moderation, calms their fears by arguing that the wise profit most from the lessons of the enemy and quickens their interest with the promise of great benefits.

Once they have agreed to listen to Pisthetaerus, the birds reveal several other characteristics. Hoopoe has already suggested they are stupid and easy to manipulate. Now, in mistrusting men whose

cleverness seems as dangerous as that of wolves or foxes, they admit
their own lack of wit. But their ambition exceeds even their fear.
Desperate for self-pride and status, they readily accept the proofs of
their former greatness. They desire to extend their power, but they
utterly lack the cunning to recognize that they can be a very real
threat to both men and gods. They need Pisthetaerus to plan, guide,
and encourage the enterprise. The birds are, in effect, the
democratic mob, seething with energy, ambition, and the need for
self-definition, but powerless without a leader because they have
neither the organization or political acumen necessary for effective
action. In lines 637 - 38, the chorus leader hands his troops over to
Pisthetaerus just as the Allies placed themselves under the control of
Athens after the Persian Wars.

> We await your orders, sir. Tasks that need
>   more brawn and muscle
> We birds can do. The complicated mental
>   stuff we leave to you.
>   (Arrowsmith, trans.)

They are putty in the hands of Pisthetaerus who proves, with a
ludicrous and punning parody of Aesop's cosmogony, that they existed before Saturn, the Titans, and Earth. He then caps his learned
explanations with the lessons of experience—birds, perched on
kings' scepters, direct nations and even rule the seasons and the
days, as everyone from farmer to Zeus himself acknowledges. As his
examples here satirize familiar symbols of power, so his political advice satirizes contemporary military strategy. The enemy can be
starved into submission with a "Melian famine" (l. 186), a direct
reference to Athens' cold-blooded destruction of the neutral island
of Melos the year before. Or one can charge gods for passing
through the birds' territory on their way to earth or demand a piece
of the sacrifice which men send up to Olympus. Threats to destroy
the food supply can be coupled with bribes of health, wealth, and
long life. All these tactics were used and reused in the course of this
and previous wars. The birds are ecstatic. They have been promised
the easy fulfillment of all their desires.

While the humans go in to get their wings, the birds address the
audience. Unlike other comic choruses, they never drop their
dramatic character or break the illusion of the plot. Instead they
draw the spectators directly into the comedy by attempting to
recruit them as citizen-subjects. They ape Pisthetaerus' best

rhetorical techniques, but then they add some clever arguments of their own. Using a more elaborate and lyrical cosmogony, they try to prove that they are indeed more ancient deities than the Olympians. They offer to make the audience citizens of their bird-city, permitting each of them freedom to be whatever kind of bird he chooses, since a corresponding bird species exists for every conceivable human aberration. The audience is treated to a list of the uses and pleasures of wings, some specifically attractive to spectators, for example, the freedom to fly away from a boring tragedy or to go defecate and get back in time for the comedy.

By the second parabasis (l. 1058), they are confident of their divinity. They no longer need to convince. Instead, they demand a sacrifice from the audience and then proclaim a price on the head of their enemy the bird seller, modeled on an Athenian proclamation against a recently condemned atheist. Even though apotheosized, the birds must persuade their worshippers to reward this comedy. Their metaphor for the contest, the Judgment of Paris, equates the audience with the hero who must decide among divinities. Thus when the birds become gods, the spectator-subjects become themselves heroic. In the last section of the play some human individuals actually acquire wings and thus become bird-gods too. Therefore, the entire group of spectators, through communication with the chorus and identification with the actors, participates in the fantasy which reveals their kinship with birds and thus with the divine.

Other characteristics of the birds are developed in the parabasis and following parts of the comedy. Their magnificent lyricism is displayed throughout in the elaborate rhythms borrowed from the poetry of Pindar, Bacchylides, and the tragedians, and punctuated by beautiful bird sounds. Their apotheosis is underlined metrically; the anapests, their leitmotif, become more stately as the play progresses. The birds express themselves with poetic diction, vivid imagery, and extended metaphor—in marked contrast to the pragmatic, precise words of Pisthetaerus and the banal comments of his friend. Free to roam the earth and soar through the sky, the birds also possess superior knowledge of life's mysteries. They have witnessed strange wonders like the secrets of the thief Orestes or the necromancers Socrates and Chaerephon. They display this lyricism and omniscience in the brilliant description of the tree named for the coward and informer, which blossoms with slander in the fall and sheds its shield in the spring.

The birds' attitude toward themselves and their environment changes with their status and as mortals become aware of the potential for pleasure in bird life. Once delighted with a pure and simple pastoral existence, the birds now boast of their power to go anywhere and do anything, particularly to satisfy their bodies' needs with inpunity. They entice mortals to join them by promising freedom from legal and moral codes, since the shameful acts men perform are natural among certain birds. Their delight in life is not confined to sexual pleasure, however. Now that they have been politicized by Pisthetaerus, they become an energetic, skillful group of activists, capable of repeating their leader's words and effecting his schemes. The messenger reports that the wall has been constructed by an efficient and cooperative unit organized to perform labors for which they are naturally equipped. And they snap to their leader's commands, joyfully accepting his right to rule them and enjoy the benefits of his supremacy. They have become, in effect, the ideal citizenry, satisfied with themselves, useful to the state, and respected by their leaders.

If the birds become citizens as well as divinities, their home becomes the city par excellence. The lofty name Cloud-Cuckoo-Land identifies the location and inhabitants while suggesting the whimsy and humbug by which it was founded. But the scene after the first parabasis establishes the city in the sky as an allegory of Athens. The city selects Athena as patroness, contains a Pelargic Wall, such as surrounded the Acropolis in Athens, and includes the Chians, the Athenians' most faithful ally, in its prayers for prosperity. The constant stream of people that clamor for entry dramatizes both the vitality and the pressure of life in busy Athens. Some are only nuisances; scenes with the priest, the poet, the oracle monger, and the scientist allow the comedian to ridicule the affectations of those who profess to have superior skills and knowledge. Others, like the inspector, the dealer in decrees, and the informer are clearly Athenian parasites on the public, hard to get rid of and productive of nothing but profit to themselves and trouble to others. It is ironic that Pisthetaerus and Euelpides find the quiet place they were seeking, only to turn it into the city they have fled. Certainly this twist must be a wry comment on the madness of contemporary Athenians or, perhaps, on the social needs of human nature.

Cloud-Cuckoo-Land is not exactly the same as Athens, however. Once the ambience of urban life has been established by the throngs that rush in and out and the comic possibilities of each type have been exhausted, Pisthetaerus has both the freedom and the power to use the people as he pleases. He treats the poets gently, forcefully ejects the informer, and converts the potential parricide's hostility into an acceptable social action. Thus, Cloud-Cuckoo-Land is Athens idealized—purged of undesirables, containing a perfect citizenry, and a clever leader. Most important, the comic hero, powerless in Athens, has placed himself in full control of Cloud-Cuckoo-Land.

All that remains is for the entire city to be apotheosized by the capitulation of the gods to the realities already established in earth and sky. Three fast-moving scenes demonstrate the physical and intellectual triumph over the Olympians. First, the messenger goddess Iris is intercepted on her way to demand sacrifices from mortals. She is insulted, nearly raped, and is finally sent back to Olympus to announce that all sacrifices now belong to the birds, who are fully prepared to destroy Zeus if he protests. Next, Prometheus sneaks down, hidden by an umbrella, to describe the starvation and near-anarchy to which the gods have been reduced. Ever a traitor, he advises them to demand Zeus' scepter and Basileia, his royal housekeeper, from the embassy that will come to sue for peace. Pisthetaerus shrewdly outwits the trinity from Olympus—Poseidon, Heracles, and Triballos the barbarian god. At first, he blithely ignores them to cook a gourmet dish which wins over the gluttonous Heracles before negotiations even begin. When Poseidon refuses to concede Basileia and the scepter, Pisthetaerus changes his tactics, arguing the advantage of bird divinity to Poseidon and citing Athenian laws of illegitimacy to prove that Heracles the bastard will inherit nothing from Zeus. Triballos must break the tie, but when Heracles and Poseidon cannot agree on the translation of his pigeon Greek, Pisthetaerus interprets in his own favor to gain the scepter and the royal bride.

The chorus' last songs hail Pisthetaerus as golden bridegroom, victorious general, and the highest of the gods, dispenser of thunder and lightning. Thus the man who first appeared on the stage as an exile, lost and without family, has fulfilled the private and public fantasies of all men. He has a luscious sex partner and the supreme command over men, and even controls nature. In the beginning, he is barely distinguishable from Euelpides. They engage in similar comic patter and exhibit the same fears. But a distinction between the two gradually emerges. It is Pisthetaerus who suggests going to the birds, imaginatively transforms the pole of heaven into the *polis* ("city") in the sky, and plans the strategy for expansion to empire. Euelpides cannot keep pace with him. He lacks the brains as well as the courage to defend himself against the beaks of the bird chorus. While Pisthetaerus constructs ingenious arguments to convince the birds to implement his plan, Euelpides can only clinch the arguments with banal comments from his own experience. On the one hand, this is a familiar comic technique which heightens the humor by emphasizing the ludicrousness of the evidence. But it also serves to separate Pisthetaerus from the common herd, bird or man. He is the hero; soon after the parodus, he stands alone, without even Hoopoe.

If his superiority is clear, so too is his will to power. Once he is in control, he takes over completely, barking out commands to all, insulting his servants, and peremptorily relegating his friend to the dirty work while he supervises from a lofty position. He uses his complete freedom to get as much as he can for himself. Yet, the birds worship him as a god for having directed them to their glorious destiny while the mortals on earth have awarded him a golden crown for wisdom and seek to emulate him. In the end, he has obtained Zeus' power to destroy everything, perhaps even his own followers. (Arrowsmith sees a sinister suggestion in the menu for the nuptial feast—roast bird).[14] The implication is that for the ruled, little has really changed but the ruler. The comic hero's wish fulfillment parallels the demagogue's as well as the demos'.

IV *Equality and Apotheosis*

There is only a slight hint of the sinister, however. Rather the whole play seems to be a celebration of man's harmony with nature. This arises from the correlation between humans and birds, at first metaphorically and then literally. The matching of bird species to human types provides lampoons, puns, and imagery throughout the play. In addition, opposing characteristics blend gradually as the drama progresses. The humans have sought out the birds to find a simple pastoral existence in nature. Interestingly enough, the word for pasture is *nomos*, whereas the word for nature is, of course, *physis*. As Whitman has pointed out, Aristophanes develops the ambiguities in these two terms when bird and human nature confront each other.[15] *Nomos* provides a number of associations for both groups. With one accent, the word means law or song; with a different accent, it means pasture or bird haunt. The playwright actually puns on the two meanings in several places (ll. 1286, 1343, 1346). In the beginning, bird life is described as a veritable honeymoon with bountiful nature providing free pasture for all, unlike Athens where the citizen is oppressed by debts, laws, and thieves. The antithesis is upset when the supposedly gentle birds violently attack the humans only to discover that they have much in common with them. The birdbrains turn out to be every bit as political as the men. Already possessed of a military organization and speech, all they need is a clever leader to direct their ambition and energy toward political action.

Moreover, the birds are no more virtuous than the humans; certain species are as violent and degenerate as certain men. And, to attract prospective citizens, the birds advertise the absence of law and shame in birdland. If the birds appear to be dupes, easily manipulated by clever humans who know exactly what will appeal to them, then the mortals, identified with the spectators, are no less easily convinced. Just as the birds eagerly became imperialists, so the mortals, ever followers of the latest trend, imitate the manners of birds and storm the gates of Cloud-Cuckoo-Land seeking wings. Thus the "pastoral" birds are seen to have the   same social characteristics as man, and man's dubious nature is thereby justified by identification with the gorgeous creatures that appear on stage.

At the beginning, the birds seem to have two other characteristics that man cannot share—music and freedom. Both are associated with the word *nomos*, for music belongs to the free-flying birds, whereas men are restrained by law and custom. The best symbol for freedom, however, is the possession of wings, granted to the hero and offered to the audience partway through the play. For comic purposes, flying means the power to go wherever one wishes, to do whatever he wants, and to escape the consequences. But human beings have always possessed their own wings—words—as Pisthetaerus' conversation with the informer reveals,

> INFORMER
> Listen, mister: it's wings I want, not words.
>
> PISTHETAIROS
> But my words *are* wings.
>
> INFORMER
> Your words are *wings?*

PISTHETAIROS
But of course. How else do you think mankind
won its wings if not from words?

INFORMER
From words?

PISTHETAIROS
Wings from words.
You know the old men, how they loll
around at the barbershop
grousing and bitching about the
younger generation?—
"Thanks to that damned Dieitrephes
and his damned advice," growls one, "my
boy has flown the family nest to take
a flier on the horses."
"Hell,"
pipes another, "you should see that kid
of mine: he's gone so damn batty over
those tragic plays, he flies into fits
of ecstasy and gets goosebumps all over."

INFORMER
And *that's* how words give wings?

PISTHETAIROS
Right.
Through dialectic the mind of man takes
wing and soars; he is morally and spiritually
uplifted. And so I hoped with words of
good advice to wing you on your way toward
some honest trade.

(ll. 1437 - 49, Arrowsmith trans.)

This conversation makes explicit the correlation between the literal wings of birds and the soaring imaginations of men. Throughout the play figurative language has not only described the action; it has actually created it. Pisthetaerus literally goes "to the birds" and then constructs a *polis* ("city") from the pole of heaven.[16] The uniquely human ability to imagine and utter the "winged word" confers the same power as the birds' wings: to go everywhere, to experience everything, and even, as the Sophists were teaching, to escape any threatening situation. Thus here too there is a blending. The humans get their wings while the birds benefit from the human power of speech.

The fusion is also reflected in *nomos* as song. The magnificent lyricism of the bird chorus has already been noted. But the grandeur of their odes is effected through Aristophanes' imitation of the most elaborate verse forms and diction of Greek public poetry, both sacred and profane. So too is the seriousness of the situation underscored by the parody of tragic style. In the first part of the play Athenians are compared to chirping crickets, but, after the parodus, human music presents itself directly on the stage in the form of two poets, a parasite who begs clothes in exchange for eulogies and an "artiste" who pretentiously seeks grander forms of expression. Their lyrics, which are an elaborate pastiche of all the great poets since Homer, pay tribute to the tradition while mocking its excesses. For Pisthetaerus treats both poets rather gently, dressing one in warm garments and offering the other a place in Cloud-Cuckoo-Land as leader of a bird chorus. In the poets' episodes, the association between wings and human song is continued. Cinesias' silly lines suggest the beauty, truth, and holy inspiration implicit in the mysterious (or cloudy) art of poetry.[17] Cloud-Cuckoo-Land clearly belongs to the human songbirds as well as the politicians.

The human celebration of harmony with nature includes more than a fusion with birds, however. The wish fulfillment extends to union with, and even control over, cosmic forces, symbolized in Greek culture by the Olympians and their weapons. This is accomplished in several ways. On the political level, the apotheosis evolves from the strategy Pisthetaerus has borrowed from the imperialist tactics of the Greeks. He begins with the simple declaration that the birds are themselves the real divinities. According to the verbal magic of the play, words then effect aggressive acts of fortification, imposition of tribute, and blockade. When the Olympians are starved into capitulation, the winged hero's marriage to Basileia, a familiar tactic in power politics, makes him King of the Gods.

Pisthetaerus is the comic everyman, representing the potential in all of us. Thus his apotheosis is in part our own. Yet, politically, he is the ruler, ever distinct from the ruled. Therefore, we receive our vicarious divinity only through identification with his subjects. The birds makes themselves gods and then in pity for the audience, whom they describe as "ephemeral," "wingless," and "made of clay" (ll. 686 - 7), they invite the spectators not only to worship birds but to put on wings themselves. The messenger's speech and the crowd of actors flying up to Cloud-Cuckoo-Land dramatize our own apotheosis. At the sacred marriage spectators and actors, all the winged tribes of *sunnomon* ("fellow feeders"), are invited to follow the bride and groom to Olympus, to the lands and bed of Zeus himself (l. 1755 ff).

If men and birds are raised to gods, the gods are reduced to the level of mankind. The powerful, mysterious, and threatening cosmos, represented by the Olympians, is dramatized in ludicrous and completely comprehensible human terms. Modern men, shocked by parodies of religious ceremonies and ridicule of the gods themselves in Old Comedy, forget that drama was part of public worship, and perhaps a few words of explanation are required here. Anthropomorphic myth allowed the gods personalities and biographies independent of their traditional responsibility for the establishment of a just and orderly universe. Philosophers, of course, examined and sometimes exploited the contradictions. But although conceptions of divinity changed in the course of the fifth century, most men believed that the gods existed and influenced the course of human events. Atheism was a capital offense in Athens at the time the *Birds* was presented, and the desecration of the Herms just before the fleet sailed for Sicily caused fear of divine retaliation. The grandeur of tragedy testifies to the fact that the Greek humanists of the fifth century took their Olympians as seriously as they took themselves. So too does the mocking of the gods in Old Comedy, for it evolves from the carnival-like comos associated with Dionysus, a god of fertility and rebirth. In part, the celebration represents the death before life, chaos before the creation of order. The negation of divine power and the separateness of the gods in comedy is a strong testimonial to the omnipresent belief in their reality. This negation also provides a sacred release, ceremonial and therefore permitted, without guilt or punishment, and restrained by the confines of the celebration itself. The spectator who laughs at Poseidon or Heracles purges himself, at least temporarily, of his hostility to the ineluctible laws of the cosmos and his anxiety about the unknown.[18] The ridicule also purges the spectator of the guilt he feels about himself. If the gods are like men, then men, in effect, are gods too, and their own imperfections are justified by the cosmic analogue.

Aristophanes' primary technique is to portray the gods as stock comic figures. Prometheus, the coward, hides under an umbrella, a comic transformation of the reed in which he stole fire from

Heaven. His masquerade of a maiden in a public procession mocks the religious ceremony as well as the sneaky god. Poseidon and Iris are both pompous quacks, who take themselves too seriously. Pisthetaerus' crudeness destroys the lady's pretensions to dignity, whereas Poseidon's bluster gets him nowhere in the face of his enemy's cleverness. Heracles is a gluttonous buffoon, and Triballus is so dumb he cannot even speak Greek. These gods, like man, act not from principle but from private needs and desires.

Like humans, the Olympians are political animals. Pisthetaerus is able to defeat them because the gods operate from the same principles of power politics and have an organization and citizenry like Athens' own. Prometheus, divine analogue to the traitor, reveals that Basileia supervises the laws, the dockyard, the arsenals, even the public payroll. Just now, he says, the foreign gods (the democratic element) are threatening rebellion because the markets are closed and empty. Poseidon, the aristocratic brother of Zeus, laments the degeneration of the government in the throes of democracy (l. 1570). The ambassadors are well-versed in the formulas of diplomacy as well as the intricacies of the law of inheritance. In the end, Heracles acts from personal rather than public motives. The Olympian state is, in effect, shown to be as busy, fractious, and self-defeating as Athens itself.

The hedonism of men is also duplicated by the hedonism of the gods. In comedy the pleasure principle is dramatized by sexual freedom, and the gods are every bit as oversexed as humans. In art as in life, sexual license is also an indicator of power and purpose. Reasoning from the myths, Pisthetaerus implies that gods only come down to earth to seduce men's wives. He imagines them with erections and suggests putting rings on their foreskins to force submission. As ruler of the birds, however, he humiliates Iris by treating her as a sex object, saying out loud what men can only think to themselves when they ogle an attractive woman. He boasts of his own powerful erection, with satisfaction guaranteed. Pisthetaerus' rise to power climaxes in the grand finale when the hero takes Zeus' own woman to his bed. Many of the festivals, as well as other comedies, may have actually culminated in a *hieros gamos* ("sacred marriage") where the two human sex partners represent a god and goddess whose heavenly intercourse insures fertility for the coming year. Through the action of the play we are all participants in the ritual. The wedding of Pisthetaerus (Zeus) to Basileia (Hera) is symbolic of a great cosmic copulation, the union of birds, men, and gods who will share powers and pleasures without end. We must remember that three preceding tragedies have already dramatized the distance between man and god and the inevitability of death. *Birds* provides a grand conclusion to the day of worship, for through laughter, it expresses an acceptance of man's participation in nature's cycle and celebrates his ultimate divinity.

CHAPTER 6

The Battle of the Sexes:
Lysistrata (Lysistratē)

I *Summary*

ARISTOPHANES presented *Lysistrata* under the name of Callistratus at the Lenaea of 411. Unfortunately we have no idea which prize the play won. To modern audiences, however, *Lysistrata* is the most popular of Aristophanes' plays because it is most easily accessible to outsiders. It does not abound in the topical allusions and lampoons of Athenian institutions that require copious footnotes for twentieth-century readers. Instead, the action moves swiftly from plan to resolution without formal interruptions where the chorus drops its dramatic character to lecture the audience.

In 411 the citizens at the winter festival were probably not in the mood to be lectured to or to laugh at specific lampoons of themselves and their city. The situation was too serious. The Sicilian expedition had ended in disaster. The entire fleet, with the youth and resources of the empire, had been destroyed in the harbor of Syracuse in 413. In the next years, the restive allies saw their chance to break free; several had defected to the other side. To make matters worse, the Spartans, acting on the advice of Alcibiades, had occupied a strategic area near Athens and concluded a treaty with Persia. Characteristically, the Athenians refused to recognize defeat. Instead they were now reorganizing in order to recoup their losses. A board of ten *Probouloi* ("Commissioners of Public Safety") had just been appointed as an emergency substitute for the Council of Five Hundred. Chosen for their age and experience, these men were charged with taking all necessary measures to deal with the dangerous situation.

Like *Acharnians* and *Peace*, *Lysistrata* concerns a successful effort to stop the war. All three are fantasies. In 425 Dicaeopolis fights alone to attain his private peace and prosperity at a time when the

91

majority is not suffering enough to want a truce. By 421 Trygaeus flies up to Olympus to free the goddess Peace so that negotiations, being prepared in fact, can succeed at the theater. Now in 411 the fantasy has changed to match the new situation. Unlike the earlier plays, *Lysistrata* does not attack leaders and policies that have so obviously failed the citizens. Instead Aristophanes chooses females as heroes, probably because they are politically powerless in reality and even anonymous to those outside their family circle. The women do not belong in the public places and assemblies that Dicaeopolis and Trygaeus frequent. Thus the impossibility of the plot is implicit in the poet's choice of characters and scenes. Moreover, by this device, Aristophanes can direct the audience's ridicule and latent hostility away from sensitive areas of political failure toward the more general and humorous excesses of male chauvinism.

The fantasy has a further function, of course—catharsis of anxieties for all those who know that in reality peace now means total surrender. Again the choice of characters is the device which leads to audience wish fulfillment. Spartan as well as Athenian males appear as warriors ignobly defeated by their women. Thus the spectators can take comfort from the reduction of the terrifying Spartan infantry to men with erections, no different from their own soldiers. In addition, all the wives of Greece, allies and enemies, cooperate to achieve reconciliation according to Lysistrata's plan. Thus the audience sees opponents whose needs, daily lives, and even hopes and dreams are identical with their own. For the moment at least, cultural differences and past emnities seem unimportant and easy to transcend.

The plot of the play is ironic. The women of Greece, led by the Athenian heroine Lysistrata, unite to initiate a war in order to achieve peace. Their enemy is the Greek military machine which has left their beds empty. So, to regain their sex lives, they plot to abstain from sex, hoping to force their men to agree to a truce. The structure is unusually coherent. The action moves without interruption from plan through two crises to a resolution at the end. Even the choral odes are closely integrated with the episodes. While the young women bar their husbands from their treasures, the older women seize the Acropolis to exclude the men from the city treasury as well. When a chorus of decrepit old men attempts to smoke them out, a chorus of spry old ladies defends the citadel. A Proboulos, one of the Board of Ten Commissioners of Public Safety, rushes to the scene with armed Scythian policemen so that he can open the public treasury. Their attempts to drive the women off by force end in the utter humiliation of the males. Although the commissioner listens to Lysistrata's defense of the women's action and her cogent political advice, he is not persuaded. Instead he goes out to report the siege to his colleagues on the board. Meanwhile, defections from the women themselves threaten the scheme; unable to control their sex drives, the women invent excuses to escape to their homes and their men. Not deceived, Lysistrata rallies them to the cause. The success of their effort is demonstrated when one husband comes in with a giant erection and demands his wife. Using all her wiles, she stops him just short of actual penetration to force him to arrange a truce before she will allow consummation. After he leaves, a delegation of Spartans and Athenians arrive in the same state of agitation, eager to make peace and love. Lysistrata chastises both groups, forces concessions from each, and then grants them a share in the naked dancing girl, Reconciliation. The two groups share a banquet before going off toward a future of sex and harmony in a festive grand finale sung by a Spartan to Athena.

II Women in a Man's World

The sight of a female character standing before the Propylaea, or Sacred Gate to the Acropolis, preparing to convene an assembly would strike the spectators as strange indeed. For the Athenian, public places belonged to the men. Respectable women went outdoors rarely and usually only if veiled and accompanied by a maid. Wives managed their homes and families, and no doubt, received power, respect, and love within their own households, but they seem to have led very isolated lives, confined to domestic duties in female quarters.[1] The public expectations for women are perhaps best summarized by Pericles' words in the Funeral Oration quoted by Thucydides: "if I must say anything on the subject of female excellence to those of you who will now be in widowhood, it will be all comprised in this brief exhortation. Great will be your glory in not falling short of your natural character; and greatest will be hers who is least talked of among the men whether for good or for bad."[2] But Lysistrata and her followers are clearly capable of masculine organization and tactics. They convene the assembly from all over Greece, even enemy territory, occupy the Acropolis and blockade themselves against male penetration, and detain certain Spartan women as hostages. To solemnize their conspiracy, the women swear an oath which is a hilarious parody of the warriors' bloody libations on the battlefield.

But the audience is never allowed to forget that the conspirators are women. When they first imitate male actions, they are extremely self-conscious, deprecating their own weaknesses and positions as housewives. Lysistrata must show them how easily their delicate instruments from the women's quarters can be turned into weapons of war. Their language, military tactics, and tools are borrowed from the world of women, so that they remain women, even when they become soldiers. Ironically, they display the very faults men accuse them of—triviality, deceit, drunkenness, and licentiousness. Perhaps these censures had some basis in fact. Certain female celebrations of fertility cults were particularly orgiastic, and the myth about Tiresias' sex change conveys the cultural belief that women enjoyed intercourse more than men.[3] Ehrenburg suggests that their lonely lives may have driven them to drink.[4] Whatever the historical reality, the women's dual roles as wives and warriors broaden the satire of this particular Peloponnesian War to the eternal battle of the sexes, where the enemies are men rather than Spartans, and misogyny is the central issue. Moreover, peace becomes as possible, desirable, and fulfilling as a successful marriage is to both sexes.

It is important to note that these women are all wives and that sex is limited to marriage. The playwright ignores the fact that husbands could easily find relief through professional prostitutes (known as *hetaerae*) as well as in homosexual relationships which society condoned. Instead the husbands swell with desire for their wives alone and acknowledge the responsibilities of fatherhood. Males and females assume that marriage is the natural state for adults, and its interruption disturbs them enough to end the war. The political application is obvious. Sexual pleasure is inseparable from the joys and duties of family life because the stable family is the backbone of the state and the provider of future citizens. By extension, women's values—food, clothes, wine, love, and children—become associated with the survival of the state. In addition, marriage is developed into the perfect metaphor for the potential relationship between the Athenians and the Spartans. Although man and wife, like Athenian and Spartan, must recognize their inevitable differences, they are united by an identity of needs and a real desire to satisfy each other.

Despite the thematic emphasis on married love, *Lysistrata* dramatizes the power of sex *per se*. The plot of this grand eulogy of the body grows from the assumption that sexual satisfaction is a more pressing human need than lust for power. The exaggerated sexuality of the women and the obvious discomfort of the excited soldiers not only stimulate laughter but also release the very real and embarrassing feelings we try to repress but must sometimes confront. So the play abounds in humor which emphasizes the gross physical realities in the life of rational man. This humor is most obviously expressed in the sexual sight gag, the best example of which is the warriors' enormous and painful phalluses. But the poet also uses vivid descriptions of intercourse itself in the hilarious oath in the prologue, for example, where the women swear not to move in rhythm, lift their legs, or crouch on top, like a lion on a cheesegrater. Free from all inhibitions, the characters in comedy cavalierly say and do what polite society or public decorum would never permit in real life.[5] Lysistrata and her Athenians do more than compliment Spartan breasts and Athenian crotches; they actually pet them without offense. Nor do the women blush at masturbation. Rather they regret that naval disasters have cut off their supply of leather phalluses. The prologue also introduces another comic device that runs rampant through the entire play—the sex pun or double entendre. Almost every word of dialogue can be interpreted as an allusion to genitalia and lovemaking. For example, the description of women's clothes (ll. 42 - 48) refers to apparel on the literal level, but actually teems with obscene puns on positions and foreplay.[6] The ubiquity of sex in action, sight, image, and language emphasizes the theme of its power, and thus, its relation to survival and the triumph of life, so important to this peace play as well as to the festival of the fertility god Dionysus.

Although the women do not belong in the public places, they quickly identify themselves as typical comic characters. Lysistrata is as much a hero as Dicaeopolis or Trygaeus. She alone possesses the imagination capable of conceiving the fantastic plan which is destined to succeed not only by the logic of comedy but also because of her own persuasiveness, cunning, and courage. Cleonice serves as the familiar buffoon whose earthy remarks have a real purpose: to distinguish Lysistrata's intelligence while mocking the seriousness she attaches to herself. The oversexed Cleonice finds a sexual innuendo in Lysistrata's most serious speeches. Myrrhine seems to be the youngest of the three Athenians since it is she who later dramatizes the power of sex.[7] The arrival of the other women provides an opportunity for good-natured, if obscene, lampoons of national characteristics: the fertile bushes of the Boeotians, callipygeous Corinthians, the women from Anagyros who still smell of this morning's lovemaking. Both the Athenians and the foreigners are revealed to have similar lives and interests—home, children, and SEX, SEX, SEX. Interestingly enough, Lysistrata has a double, the Spartan Lampito who immediately comprehends the scheme, helps to persuade the other women, and succeeds in effecting in Sparta what Lysistrata accomplishes in Athens. The lampoons of her are almost complimentary: gentle mocking of her Laconian dialect as well as lecherous praise for the healthy complexion and strong body her gymnastic education has produced. Lampito's presence in the prologue and her affinities with Lysistrata help to humanize the enemy and make the wish fulfillment plausible.

As the conspirators disperse, a chorus of decrepit old men enters dragging smudgepots to smoke the intruders out of the Acropolis. If one believes their boasts, they have participated in all the major victories of Athens and are over one hundred years old.[8] The chorus of old women who repel their attempt call them "walking corpses" and "refugees from the tomb." The females are far spryer, but they too lament the pains and burdens of old age. This is a familiar complaint in the earlier comedies, too. As is to be expected, the victory of Lysistrata's plan will bring about the defeat of old age. When these choruses lay aside their enmity, they will gain youthful vigor and sexual desire as well as peace.

In the parodus, however, they are bitter enemies and the area before the Acropolis is their battlefield. The men shout violent physical threats and employ typical masculine weapons of destruction like torches and battering rams. The women turn their meeting place, the well, into their armory and use water pitchers to put the fire out, while their insults come from the kitchen and the laundryroom. The situation in the prologue, where the encounter between the sexes is expressed metaphorically in military terms, is here reversed. The choruses are too old to seduce or rape, but their fighting suggests the sex act. The males threaten to penetrate the Acropolis with hard flaming sticks. Clearly the gates of the citadel represent the female gates of love shut tight against any warrior's phallus. Both fire and water are destructive elements here, but, as the opponents grow less hostile, their armaments will take on new connotations associated with love, regeneration, and nurture.

The women have just drenched the men when a commissioner

from the Board of Ten enters accompanied by four policemen. Because he needs money to pay the fleet, he is on his way to recapture the treasury. Like other males, he plans a forced entry; he will pry open the gates with a crowbar. Lysistrata and a few followers emerge of their own free will, however. The police who attempt to seize them are beaten back with vegetables, fruits, and bread. Having triumphed as warriors, the women move on to politics to demonstrate their acumen with analogies from household management and weaving. The men are not persuaded, but they are defeated. The commissioner retreats, soaked to the skin like the chorus, dressed as both a woman and a corpse being prepared for his funeral.

The humor of the episode depends on several familiar elements. The commissioner is that ridiculous figure, the quack, whose pretentiousness must be deflated by those around him. Preposterously confident of his male superiority, he condemns all women as lushes, lechers, and religious fanatics. He even blames one wife for the entire Sicilian disaster. Of course, he approves of beating wives to keep their doors and their mouths shut. But the whole cult of masculine physical superiority is dealt a deathblow in the episode. A barrage of vegetables repels the armed policemen who defecate from fear as they run. The elaborate armor and uniforms of the warriors lose their power to impress when men are described as using their helmets as soupbowls and their spears to steal figs. By the end, the Proboulos is utterly emasculated; veiled and gowned, he becomes just what he has insulted.

This episode not only ridicules male dependence on force, it also questions assumptions about their monopoly of intellect and patriotism. The women prove that they have made the supreme sacrifice for the state; they are giving up sex for peace just as before they were called upon to give up sons and husbands for war. Lysistrata's criticisms of politics and her own platform do more than demonstrate the females' ability to understand issues and develop policy. When she compares the art of governing to her own skills in household management and wool carding, she, in effect, belittles the belief that men's work is so much more difficult and important than women's. Lysistrata's triumph over this anonymous Proboulos releases the audience's hostility against politicians and warmongers without directing attention to specific negative criticism. Instead, the faults all males have in common are ridiculed by the comparison with womanly skills and virtues.

The leaders of the warring choruses have participated in the episode by encouraging their respective sexes. Moving with the actors, they too extend their battle from physical attack to political rivalry. In the next ode, the men accuse the women of a plot to reestablish tyranny with the help of Sparta. They promise to squelch them just as they helped destroy Athens' former tyrants. The women respond by enumerating their services to the state. Unlike the men who have wasted lives and money, they have bestowed beauty and joy on the people. The heated argument threatens to descend to blows again. Both sides strip naked for action with angry words that blend politics with sex.

This ode is the only choral section in the play that resembles a parabasis. Both choruses remove their cloaks here, to reveal nakedness instead of fancy costumes, and the women address the audience as citizens directly. But there is no interruption of the dramatic illusion. Instead the spectators are encouraged to become part of the play by the realistic tone of the arguments on both sides. The women defend their right to express political opinions by recalling their important contributions to public festivals where the citizens have worshiped. The men's response echoes the repressed fears of males everywhere that women will usurp their perquisites. Characteristically, the men's chorus dispels the threat by reducing females to sex objects, as in their translating the thought of women on horseback into a demeaning joke about intercourse. Political charges and countercharges rally the audience behind one sex or the other. The females, however, clinch their argument with a point which unites everyone—actors, chorus, and audience; all lust after Boeotian eels (an image with phallic overtones [cf. l. 36]), the symbol of all the worldly pleasures the war has deprived them of. Thus, the stage battle of the sexes becomes directly relevant to the spectators because they share the same attitudes and desires.

Before the fighting begins, Lysistrata emerges from the Acropolis declaiming misogynist sentiments in tragic style. She is discouraged because as she herself admits, "In short, we want to get fucked" (l. 715). The women are all trying to desert. Their excuses for having to return home reveal their desperation. One needs to spread her wool out on the bed while another simply must strip her flax. A third simulates pregnancy with the helmet of Athena. Her conversion of the warrior goddess' armor into a bowl for giving birth not only emasculates militarism, but also suggests that the very weapons of destruction could be tools of survival instead. Their excuses all serve as reminders that these oversexed Amazons are also respectable wives with responsibilities to their households and families. Lysistrata prevents the defection by interpreting an oracle as a promise that women can lie atop their mates after victory.

While the actors return to the Acropolis, the two choruses sing another lyric. The battle has reached a new stage. Instead of attacking with blows, the men hurl an abusive song about a famous misogynist and the women respond with a countertale about Timon the misanthrope who loved females. Then two individuals tentatively approach each other in a duet of insults and threats that reveals growing sexual desire. Thus, again the choral interlude closely parallels the action.

The shrewdness of Lysistrata's plan is proved in the next episode and ode. First Myrrhine's husband Cinesias rushes in bringing their child and a painful erection. Although Myrrhine longs to satisfy him, Lysistrata reminds her of the oath and encourages her to tease her husband to a truce. While the scene pokes fun at the male ego, feminine wiles, and the humiliating urgency of sex, several other important themes are brought out. First of all, the couple is married and clearly in love. Both miss each other as much as they miss sex and do not seriously consider satisfaction by other means. Moreover, Cinesias the warrior appreciates his home and his wife's management of it. Everything has fallen apart without her. His use of the child is comic, of course, but its presence does reinforce the association between marriage and survival. As Cinesias exits, a Spartan herald and an Athenian delegation rush in trying to hide their enormous erections. Both Lampito and Lysistrata have succeeded. The agonized men hasten to arrange peace negotiations.

The male chorus leader, in sympathy for the suffering soldiers, declares his hatred of women but the female chorus leader uses her gentle maternal ministrations to soften his anger. After she has dressed him in a warm cloak, removed a bug from his eye, and kissed him, he admits it's impossible to live with or without women and submits to peace. Then the two choruses cement their unity by singing together. Their remaining ode concerns the joys of domestic life: banquets, elegant clothes, and the cancellation of debts.[9] Now they sing directly to the audience. Each strophe begins with a generous offer to share their good fortune, but unexpectedly they renege in the last line. This humorously demonstrates the balance between public pose and private selfishness in families and states. The stand of unity against the outsider is just what Lysistrata will recommend to the Spartans and Athenians in their dealings with the barbarian.

The last scene contains the joyous grand finale familiar from earlier plays. A Spartan envoy and an Athenian magistrate enter, unable to conceal or endure their huge erections. Anticipating their haste, Lysistrata emerges with the naked goddess Reconciliation while the men stare in agony. The goddess is the personification of both plot and theme; she symbolizes the force that brought them to submission as well as all the joy of peace. But the soldiers cannot be relieved before a formal ceremony which includes purification, a shared supper, and a public exchange of oaths. While a magistrate comes out of the banquet to eulogize drunkenness, the choruses change costumes and return in new roles as Athenian and Spartan men. Thus, in the exodus, the political implications of the metaphor of the battle of the sexes become explicit. Husbands and wives, Athenians and Spartans, dance off toward their marriage beds while a Spartan praises joint actions and invokes a Spartan Athena.

III   Unisex and Peace

Lysistrata's plan to make peace depends on her assumption that men and women, Athenian and Spartan, all have common sex drives which are stronger even than their lust for power. This theme is expressed ironically throughout the play. The women make war for peace, abstain from sex to obtain it, and become more masculine to assert domestic values. The exchanging of roles and blending of images suggests that similarities between men and women, like those between enemies, are really stronger than the obvious differences.

The theme is clearest in the blending of sex roles, particularly in the women's increasing masculinity. Although their feminine qualities are never absent, the male characters learn to respect the women as warriors and politicians able to accomplish what male leadership could not even envision. Lysistrata withstands threats and insults to emerge in complete control of international affairs. She is hailed as the most manly of all by the male chorus leader who encourages her to make the best truce by being the best of both sexes (ll. 1108 ff.) As the women achieve success, the males become feminized and lose the physical and intellectual superiority that separates them from the women. The gowned and veiled magistrate is a precursor of the totally immobilized warriors, defeated by their own virility. Lysistrata insists that the Athenian husbands behave like women and lead the Spartans to her gently. Drunkenness, a prime vice of women at the beginning, is praised as the catalyst to dialogue, friendship, and happiness at the end by a male public official. All the characters exit in the joyous religious ecstasy formerly condemned as female fanaticism.

Even in the cosmos, the most important divinities are female, and a higher harmony is achieved in the fusion of masculine and feminine characteristics.[10] Lysistrata rebukes the women for calling on Zeus because she says he is helpless. (l. 716). Instead, they appeal to their own goddesses: Aphrodite, the goddess of love, and Artemis and Athena, chaste warrior goddesses who are also patrons of childbirth and weaving respectively. Pan, Bacchus, and Aphrodite are identified in the prologue with the trivial pursuits of women, but these are the very divinities whose gifts to man effect the truce. The hymns in the exodus connect the other Olympians to the ecstatic rites of fertility. The Spartan's last song actually focuses on the female divinities the two Greek nations worship in common, the Muses and Athena. The political union forged between Athens and Sparta on earth seems to reflect the harmony inherent in the cosmos, for the same warrior goddess who protects the Athenian Acropolis is cherished in the Bronze Temple at Sparta.

The images associated with each sex also begin to change as the play progresses. The women's household becomes an armory when they have to fight for peace. Everything from a diaphanous gown to an onion can be used on the battlefield if one chooses violence instead of love. The woman who wants to give birth in Athena's bronze helmet implies that the reverse is also true. The men's weapons are all violent phallic symbols—the flaming torch of the chorus, the crowbar of the Proboulos, and the spears of the warriors. But the real phallus, called a Spartan cudgel / message staff by the embarrassed herald, literally emerges as the instrument of peace and love. The fire and water that the choruses use as weapons in the parodus change their meaning in the course of the action. The men's fire becomes associated with the flames of passion, common to both sexes, and the warmth of female nurturing, perhaps best symbolized by the wool Lysistrata speaks of and the cloak the female chorus leader wraps around her shivering enemy.[11] The women's water, which puts the fire out, symbolizes the sexual abstention that is so destructive of life. But water, too, becomes ambiguous, related to passion in the old men's tears, regeneration in the ritual purification before the banquet, and the joy of life in the description of the dances by the beautiful rivers of Sparta. The fusion does not negate the potential for destruction and hostility. The magistrate still brandishes a flaming torch against the chorus, whereas Athena remains a warrior goddess. But it does dramatize the possibility of finding common ground on which to build a lasting relationship.

Like the other peace plays, *Lysistrata* reveals that making love is more fun than making war. But it is difficult to assign to Aristophanes a policy which he seriously advocates to the citizens of Athens in 411. Lysistrata's advice is only a general recommendation for ejecting the bad citizens from power and using the best most efficiently. Very little of the satire is really topical. The old men draw their examples of tyranny and treachery from the distant past, whereas Lysistrata and the Spartan praise the cooperation of the two states long before the Peloponnesian War. There are only a few references to contemporary events and people. Those politicians who do appear are anonymous representatives of both states who support no policy except male supremacy and are reduced at the end to acknowledging their debt to women. The audience, frustrated by events, is able to enjoy the humiliation of the powerful without taking the criticism too seriously or dwelling on the present. In fact, as men and women or husbands and wives, they participate in the battle of the sexes and thus enjoy the final triumph of both sides. The play deals with the deepest desire of the Athenians in 411 for peace with honor and shows how, in comedy at least, their goal is not only possible, but even in the nature of things.

CHAPTER 7

Playgirls and Poets:
Thesmophoriazousai

I Summary

T *hesmophoriazousai* was probably produced in 411, the same year as *Lysistrata,* but at the later spring festival, the City Dionysia.[1] The play concerns the same subject as *Lysistrata,* the battle of the sexes. But, instead of developing that war to satirize war and politics in general, *Thesmophoriazousai* concentrates on women in their own world, in order to avoid political problems entirely. Its setting is a women's festival where the only representatives of the government are minor officials called to expel a male intruder. Its satire focuses on the state of contemporary drama, mocking tragic playwrights as misogynists and transvestites while parodying their plot devices, spectacle, diction, and music. Thus, its subject is certainly far removed from the political realities of the spring of 411. Throughout the winter, the Athenian generals at Samos had been negotiating in secret with Alcibiades. He promised that the Persians would subsidize the Athenian war effort if they would agree to suspend the democratic constitution and establish a more stable government. The oligarchic conspirators combined political machinations with intimidation and murder so effectively that by summer the terrorized populace actually voted out the democracy. At the Lenaea in early Feburary, Aristophanes could dramatize Lysistrata confronting an anonymous commissioner from the transitional Board of Ten because the general populace was probably not yet aware of the plot. By April, however, suspicion and fear must have been rampant.[2] Therefore, for safety's sake, as well as to distract his troubled audience, the playwright left politics out of this comedy.

The complicated Greek title *Thesmophoriazousai* simply means *Women at the Thesmophoria,* an all-female festival in honor of the

103

grain goddesses, Demeter and Persephone. Dudley Fitts calls it
Ladies' Day. As part of this year's proceedings, the women intend
to vote a punishment for Euripides, the tragic playwright who has
exhibited their glaring faults in the theater. But the tragedian who
delights in portraying liars, adultresses, and child murderers, has
heard of their plan and constructs a counterplot: he will send in an
infiltrator to defend him against their charges. When the young
effeminate poet Agathon refuses to go, Euripides' own father-in-law
Mnesilochus heroically volunteers. He is shaved and dressed to fool
the women, but his imposture is discovered when he insists
Euripides has revealed only a small part of their sinfulness. Once he
is exposed in public and painfully fettered, Euripides, true to an
oath, tries to save him, in hilarious parodies of rescue scenes from
his own tragic plays, *Helen* and *Andromeda*. Unfortunately, his
elaborate artistry does not succeed. He is forced to negotiate directly with the women. They agree to release Mnesilochus if he will
give up his attacks and can elude the Scythian guard. Borrowing a
plot from low life and comedy, he stages a seduction scene. While a
flute girl distracts the policeman, Euripides and Mnesilochus retreat
in haste. The women send the guard in the wrong direction and
then exit themselves, as if returning home from the festival.

II   *Ladies and Literary Criticism*

In the prologue, Euripides and his father-in-law enter in haste.[3]
The relative is too old to keep up with the poet. When he complains
and begs to be told where they are going, Euripides responds with
an irrelevant paradox and an explanation of the origin of eyes and
ears, which completely confuses Mnesilochus. Here we have the
familiar confrontation of the quack whose intellectual pretensions
are reduced to absurdity by the disingenuous comments of the fool.
Their dialogue warms up the audience while establishing the
dramatic situation. It also makes clear the perspective from which
we are to view the comic distortion of real people. Aristophanes will
satirize more than the art of poetry, for Euripides' first words establish him as a member of a new elite whose intellectual superiority so theatens the ego of ordinary citizens. Like Socrates in the
Clouds, he makes oversubtle distinctions, uses the word *physis*, and
appeals to Aether as the principle of creation. Throughout the play
he and the other tragedians will use ideas, jargon, and rhetorical
devices borrowed from the Sophists. But our confidence in the

effectiveness and superiority of their ideas will be constantly under-
mined by the coarse comments and practical activity of the more
common characters who belong to comedy instead of tragedy.

The prologue also lampoons the assumption that inspired tragic
poets can penetrate and conquer the mystery of the cosmos.
Euripides and Mnesilochus are on their way to the house of
Agathon, a younger tragic poet who is the host to both Socrates and
Aristophanes in Plato's dialogue *The Symposium*. The "comic"
Euripides is very reverent as he approaches the door. Then the servant of Agathon emerges, solemnly parodying religious formulas to
silence man and nature so that the divine poet may work without
distraction. Everyone associated with tragedy behaves as if the poet
were a god. Mnesilochus refuses to worship at his door, however.
Instead, as the servant silences the winds, he farts loudly and makes
obscene references to the poet's sex life. Thus he reduces the poet to
the spectator's level while asserting his own freedom and importance.

As the servant prepares Agathon for the epiphany, Euripides explains his predicament. On this, the third day of the public festival,
the women are gathering at the temple of Demeter to condemn him
to death for maligning them in the tragedies. Mnesilochus agrees
that Euripides deserves this fate, but he thinks the scheme, to send
Agathon to the Thesmophoria dressed as a woman to speak up for
him, is very clever and clearly in his style. He is certain that
Euripides will win a prize for the artifice (ll. 87 - 94). This theatrical
terminology makes clear that the "comic" Euripides is constructing
a play within the play of Aristophanes and that its plot parodies the
devices of the real Euripides. Agathon's penetration of the Thesmophoria is called a *mechane* (the word for crane as well as device).
Thus the divine poet will function as a *deus ex machina*, the god
flown in on the crane by Euripides to conclude difficult situations.
The interpretation of the tragedian's use of this device requires a
careful study of Euripides' art and ideas as well as of the individual
plays.[4] In any case, its frequent recurrence (e.g., in the previous
year's *Helen*) makes the device worthy of parody. Although
Euripides' *deus ex machina* usually draws together all the loose
ends in his tragedies, it does not succeed in Aristophanes' comedy.
The first scheme must be abandoned for other equally useless
devices (also called *mechanai* at ll. 927 and 1132) before the final
resolution of the problem.

When Agathon appears and confronts Mnesilochus, the criticism of tragedy takes on another dimension, which may explain in part why the comic Euripides' plots fail. Agathon is wheeled out on the ekkyklema lounging on a couch dressed in a woman's clothes. His androgynous appearance utterly confuses Mnesilochus. The ionic rhythms of the song he sings suggest effeminate frenzy and passion. To account for his impersonation, the poet expounds an interesting aesthetic theory that alludes to Sophist speculation on human nature. His dress is in harmony with his thoughts; since he is placing women on the stage, he needs to adopt the nature of his characters. But Mnesilochus deflates his intellect and lampoons his effeminacy. From the confrontation it appears that the art Agathon represents has also become effeminate, i.e., no longer deals courageously with real issues. Agathon's beardless cheek and missing phallus symbolize his effeteness. He refuses to help his friend in distress, placing selfishness before valor or honor. In contrast, Mnesilochus, a comic hero, accepts the challenge. But Euripides' play demands that this virile old man be emasculated too. In a scene full of farce and slapstick, he is shaved above and below, dressed in the finery of Agathon, and sent off with instructions to control his voice. His female impersonation will not succeed, however. The problem is solved only after he and Euripides present themselves honestly, revealing their masculine identities.

The criticism of later tragedy implicit in the characterization of Agathon and Euripides is successful precisely because it is leveled within a framework that imitates and exaggerates the conventions and techniques of drama.[5] Complex plots based on intrigue and containing elaborate recognition scenes can be traced back to Aeschylus' *Libation Bearers*. But in the later plays of Euripides, the sense of inevitability surrounding the tragic action is missing. Instead the tragedian presents ingenious characters who develop the intrigue spontaneously in response to unexpected events. The audience remains in suspense until the very end. The comic Euripides parodies the plot devices of these later dramas by constructing an elaborate private intrigue which he must keep changing to meet new situations. In *Helen*, however, even the sense of the tragic has disappeared. The successful intrigue of the good characters, Helen and Menelaos, frees them from the evil Egyptian king and allows them to return to home, hearth, and happy marriage. Euripides' new interest in matters of love and marriage suggests an abandonment of seemingly insoluble public problems. The characters' confusions of gender may symbolize not only the effeteness of tragedy but also its very loss of identity, implicit in the happy endings of plays like *Helen*. Significantly, when Aristophanes places the comic Euripides in a real-life situation, the elaborate intrigues of his tragedies seem ridiculous and end in disaster.

Aristophanes also mocks the technical devices that drama uses to create illusion and emotional impact. The dependence on spectacle appears in the use of elaborate costumes and props by the poets in the course of the play. The crane, only alluded to in the prologue, flies Euripides himself into the women's assembly. The ekkyklema, tragedy's device to expose interior scenes, is used by Aristophanes to reveal Agathon himself. Agathon's composition, in which he plays both chorus and leader, parodies the structure and imagery of dramatic and religious lyric. Its meter exaggerates the exotic rhythm patterns with unusual resolutions and combinations so popular among the avant-garde composers.[6] In presenting his plea to Agathon, the comic Euripides imitates the style and diction of tragic dialogue. Less obvious are the direct allusions to lines from actual plays. Characters fling the words of the real playwright back at the comic one. Agathon excuses his refusal with the very words with which Pheres refuses to die for his son in *Alcestis;* Mnesilochus makes sure that Euripides swears with his heart as well as his tongue, avoiding the error of Phaedra's nurse in *Hippolytus*. Mnesilochus actually cites Aeschylus when he asks Agathon some embarrassing questions. Even if the spectators could not remember the sources, they would surely recognize the imitation of tragic styles and situations and laugh at the incongruity between its grandeur and the gross reality so forcefully expressed by Mnesilochus.[7] But Aristophanes' very debunking of the devices and new use of memorable phrases call attention to the artistry involved in creating an illusion in the theater. Moreover the comedian's own skill at imitation reveals his knowledge and love for his target. Thus much of the parody is also an elaborate compliment to the creative power of the artist.

Mnesilochus the transvestite now mingles with the crowd of women who enter as if on their way to the Thesmophoria. Their parodus is an elaborate parody of the opening ceremonies of a political assembly. A female herald calls the group to silence and directs the prayers of the chorus to both the goddesses of the festival and the divine protectors of the state. While the women imitate the formulas of the men, they add their own private prayers for happiness to the prayers for political prosperity. The ritual cursing of the enemy incongruously equates the domestic sinner with the public traitor; the one who proposes peace with Euripides is condemned with the same zeal as the man who would negotiate with the Persians. The juxtaposition also underlines the triviality of the women's concerns. They agonize over exposure of adultery or child substitution instead of secret conspiracies to reestablish tyranny. Perhaps Aristophanes intends to imply a relationship between domestic treacheries and political plotting or to suggest that politicians, like poets, have assumed the characters of women.

Once the formalities have been completed, the women step forward to address their own assembly, imitating the men's rhetorical devices. The first woman presents a forceful speech describing the effect of Euripides' insults on her domestic life. Always under suspicion, she has now completely lost the power to run her household or deceive her husband. The second woman, a destitute widow, charges Euripides with destroying her economic life. His blasphemies have ruined her meager business as a weaver of chaplets. The chorus' wrath is aroused by the mention of her poor fatherless children. They are ready to exact harsh revenge when Mnesilochus comes forward to insist that women are really much worse than Euripides portrayed them. His vivid testimony of adultery, secret adoptions, and even murder so angers them that they rush to attack him.

The arrival of Clisthenes, the effeminate citizen so womanly that his presence does not profane the sacred rites, changes the direction of their anger. Clisthenes interrupts a fist fight between Mnesilochus and the first orator to report the rumor that a male has infiltrated the Thesmophoria. Then Mnesilochus' imposture is literally exposed, by his phallus as well as his words. The parody of the recognition scene familiar from tragedy is clear in the series of verbal and physical investigations that lead to the shocking discovery. Clisthenes has arrived from nowhere, like a plot device operating as a symbol of Tyche (chance) in the lives of men, but the hero, like his dramatic prototype, does not submit to necessity. Instead, he responds to the new circumstances with a device stolen from Euripides' *Telephus*, also parodied by Aristophanes in the *Acharnians*. Mnesilochus seizes a child, expecting to use it as a hostage to gain his freedom. But the plan does not succeed because the baby's bunting conceals only a wineskin. The reversal of Mnesilochus' situation and fortune has arrived. He is in "tragic" danger, guarded by the enemy while a woman goes off to get a magistrate. Still he has the courage to resist. Borrowing from Euripides' *Palamedes* this time, he scratches messages for help on statues he has found in the Thesmophorion and throws them all over the theater, hoping one will reach Euripides. Singing a grandiloquent recitative to his hands and his tablets, he sits down to await rescue.[8]

The women who capture him at the Thesmophorion are very different from the amorous Amazons who capture the Acropolis for Lysistrata. Although they too are wives from respectable families, they clearly do not represent the values of married love, domestic harmony, and survival of the family and state. Instead they seem to be comic distortions of the real Euripides' female characters. Like his choruses who wander into the orchestra to verify some gossip they heard at the well, these women are interested primarily in problems of marriage, childbirth, and household management. Nor are these subjects patent metaphors for solutions to government problems. Rather, the women's talk proves Euripides' accusations. Like his Phaedras and Melanippes (l. 547), they are faithless wives. They never deny Euripides' charges but only object that his revelations have made their husbands so suspicious that they can no longer lie, steal, keep lovers, and substitute children. Like Medea, they love and hate with equal passion and demand barbarous revenge. They threaten to poison Euripides and to burn the hairs from the crotch of the traitor before they ever discover he is a male. All their references to fire and cooking suggest punishment rather than eating or celebration, and the violent shifts of meters and unusual usages in their lyrics underline their excitability.[9] Like all his heroines, including Helen, they use guile to achieve their goals.

Actually, Aristophanes is much harder on them than the real Euripides ever was. The tragedian nearly always establishes an initial sympathy for his sinful heroines before he shows how inhuman they become when overwhelmed by passion. Other heroines, like Helen or Iphigenia in Tauris, are innocent victims capable of great love and altruism who use their "women's artful treachery" (*Helen*, l. 1621) to free themselves and their loved ones from danger. Behind Aristophanes' exaggeration of the women's shamelessness, we can see the comedian's awareness of their real situation—forced into loveless marriage, completely under the control of their husbands, and dependent on the birth of male children for status and affection. But Aristophanes is most interested in the humor of Mnesilochus dressed as a woman and defending Euripides by spouting even more examples of woman's villainy. The lecherous old goat imagines hilarious scenes of adultery on the run and fake childbirth. Ironically Mnesilochus himself is surprised by the extent of their guile. A woman's trick of dressing her wineskin as a baby both proves his charge and leads to his "tragic" reversal in which he becomes a prisoner. The women, however, are not at all perturbed by the sham. Their chorus leader has already admitted that there is nothing worse than a shameless woman except women (ll. 531 - 32).

While Mnesilochus patiently awaits his rescue, the chorus turns to the audience to present the parabasis. Addressing the spectators as husbands as well as men, the chorus leader attacks them for their suspicion, jealousy, and inconsistent behavior toward their wives. Then she changes the field of battle from domestic dissension to government, comparing individuals of each sex to prove women would be superior rulers. It is all very impressive but built entirely on cleverness with words rather than criticism of policy. The women mentioned are those whose very common names are puns for such political successes as "Victory at Sea" and "Good Government", while the well-known men who are measured against them are named without specific comment. The summary arguments on men's inferiority are based on the claim that all men commit the same sins as women, but on a much grander scale. The parabasis concludes with a reproach against men couched in typically female terms of social status. Their protest that mothers should be honored or punished in accordance with the value of the citizens they produce belittles the state system of public honors. It also provides an opportunity for political lampoon, but only of Lamachus and Hyperbolus, two familiar targets of political satire, one of whom was dead and the other certainly powerless by 411.

In the next episodes the poet and his relative attempt to effect a real escape by playing out Euripides' famous rescue scenes. The first is from *Helen* where Mnesilochus, already dressed as a woman, plays the faithful wife to Euripides' Menelaos who has been washed ashore in Egypt just as she is about to be forced to marry its barbarous king.[10] The couple's recognition scene and tender reunion parody Euripides' sentimental treatment of a common situation (cf. *Electra, Iphigeneia in Tauris, Ion*). The romantic fiction with its exotic setting is rendered ludicrous by the female guard's insistence on Mnesilochus' real situation. She even mocks the conventions that the audience normally accepts, by reducing the common stage symbol for the tomb of Proteus, at which Mnesilochus/Helen says he weeps, to the altar it really is.[11] In character and speech, she is modeled on the portress Menelaos meets in front of the Egyptian palace. When an Athenian magistrate and a Scythian guard approach, however, Euripides abandons the romantic scene and runs away. While Mnesilochus is taken in to be fettered for public exhibition, the women resume their celebration of the mysteries of the great goddesses, singing the joys of marriage and nature rather than the evils of men.

The sight of Mnesilochus chained to a post suggests a new intrigue to Euripides. He signals his father-in-law to act Andromeda to his Perseus, the hero of a lost play performed at the same festival as *Helen*.[12] Mnesilochus sets the scene himself by parodying the lament Andromeda sang as she was about to be devoured by a sea monster. The humor arises from the old man's frequent shifts from the fiction that he is Andromeda to the reality of his own situation. To heighten the effect, Aristophanes quotes passages from Euripides' text with substitutions that apply only to the father-in-law. The song's elaborate mixture of rhythms parodies Euripidean metrical technique as well. Euripides is heard first from offstage, playing Echo, his Andromeda's sole companion, whose repetitions of the heroine's laments increased the pathos of the tragic scene. In the comedy, however, the poet simply echoes the vulgarities of his impatient relative. When Euripides finally enters as Perseus, probably on the crane, he bursts into a love song at the sight of the piteous maiden chained to a rock. The Scythian policeman reacts like the woman in the previous episode. At first he tries to make sense of Euripides / Perseus' words, but then he deflates the illusion by insisting on the criminality and the maleness of the love object. Conceding in tragic style that he is wasting his innovations on a fool, the poet flees the Scythian's lash, promising to return with a new plot more suitable to a barbarian.

This time Euripides returns as himself, a poet gowned in the robe of tragedy and carrying a lyre. His new device is frankness with the women. He explains the situation, identifies the actor, and proposes a peace treaty, offering never again to malign females if they free his father-in-law. The women accept, but direct him to eject the Scythian guard. For this purpose, Euripides has brought along new tricks—a dancing girl and a flute player borrowed from the carnival-like endings of comedy. He directs them in a seduction scene to which the Scythian responds as if he had read the script. Mistaking Euripides' tragic robe for a woman's dress, he assumes the poet is a procuress and bargains for his pleasure. Euripides allows him to take the dancing girl away so he and his father-in-law can escape. When the Scythian discovers he has been duped, he angrily rushes off in pursuit, in the wrong direction. The chorus then leaves the stage with a brief exodus song indicating that the festival has concluded.

In the finale, the tragedian has turned comedian; he gets a happy ending by using farce, slapstick, and dirty tricks instead of his own more intellectual devices. In addition, Euripides has become as androgynous as Agathon. Although he admits he is a man, he is judged a female by that supermale, the Scythian policeman. Thus, the metaphor for the emasculation of tragedy is carried through to the end.

III   *Emasculation as a Metaphor*

The presentation of the new poets as transvestites implies that Aristophanes believed that pure tragedy and pure comedy lay at opposite poles, one masculine and one feminine. The metaphor of gender was a natural means for the comic poet to express the distinction between the two forms. Women were without legal rights as individuals or citizens and were limited to domestic duties thought appropriate to their passionate natures and maternal instincts. Men were assumed to be more rational and ambitious. Thus they inherited the responsibility for governing society and were free to fully develop their powers and explore the boundaries of human experience. Pure tragedy could be viewed as masculine because it is concerned with noble men whose extraordinary deeds affect the lives of their communities and whose destined failures lead to the perception both of man's greatness and his limitations. Without compromise tragedy sets the human action against the awesome background of the mysterious, incomprehensible, but ultimately just cosmos. The genre requires the presentation of a conventional story in a logical structure which reflects the pattern of probability and necessity in life in order to dramatize the inevitability of defeat and death. And, as Aeschylus insists in the *Frogs*, the seriousness of the subject and the grandeur of the vision demand elegant diction, rhythm, and metaphor.

Comedy is the opposite, or feminine, for many reasons. In the first place, it deals with common men in trivial situations. Although comedy frequently focuses on important public problems, it views them from the perspective of the bedroom, kitchen, or privy, and expresses them in the diction, metaphors, and rhythms of daily life. Comic heroes, whether male or female, represent universal human characteristics; they are the embodiment of the cliché, "we're all the same with our pants down." And comic characters actually strut about "with their pants down," displaying phalluses, or boasting of their breasts, buttocks, and belches. For comedy concentrates on a different truth about the human condition—the survival of the species through its connection with nature, fertility, and the eternal cycle of death and rebirth. Thus, in order to emphasize this triumph over the limitations of probability and necessity, comedy is founded on the unexpected, the improbable, and the irrational so that its stories are original creations rather than mythic reenactments, and its characters succeed through instinct and cunning rather than high moral principle or rational programs. Moreover, Old Comedy glories in human sexuality, the means to survival. Although Greek women were socially inferior, segregated and treated as sex objects or domestic servants, female characters are an indispensable part of Old Comedy. The mean but nurturing tasks women performed are central to the comic vision of human survival. In *Lysistrata* and *Ekklesiazousai*, heroines, not heroes, plot and carry out the comic action. In most other comedies, the hero's victory is not complete without the presence of a naked woman who symbolizes the pleasure and productivity possible in all human lives.

As a literary critic, Aristophanes uses the metaphor of gender to accuse Euripides of replacing the masculine dignity of tragedy with a new bastardized form. Through transvestite characters and plays within a play, the comic poet satirizes the new directions in tragedy—myths with little relevance to public affairs, women as heroines, complicated intrigue, elaborate use of spectacle, innovative music that threatens to overshadow the words, and happy endings in which ordinary human beings triumph over an indifferent universe. In part, the comedian is making a professional joke. Tragedy, once as distinct from comedy as male from female, has been encroaching on the territory of its opposite. So the mock tragic situation has a happy ending when the poet himself renounces his own high art and resorts to the low tricks of Old Comedy.

The bastardized form never becomes comedy, however. Nor do

the emasculated poets become the kind of women who represent the life-sustaining values of feminity, as Lysistrata's followers do. Rather they resemble the ladies at the Thesmophoria. Both the poets and the playgirls depend upon illusion, disguise, pretense, and deceit instead of the courage, honesty, and pragmatic ingenuity of the comic hero. Significantly, Mnesilochus, the true comic hero, is the most virile; even when dressed as a woman, he is never emasculated.

The confrontation between the poet / playgirls and the stock characters of Old Comedy dramatizes the failure of new tragedy to present insights into the truth of the human condition. In every episode their triviality is pitted against the common sense and candor of their vulgar interlocutors. Of course, these are familiar comic scenes: the confrontation between the quack and the fool or the incongruity of tragic styles in comic situations. But here more than elsewhere, the poet emphasizes the disparity between truth and illusion. The comic characters always insist on their own identities and clearly articulate their doubts. In contrast, Agathon plays both poet and chorus and male and female, while the playgirls lie and cheat to acquire property, sex, and status. Euripides himself obscures obvious perceptions and applies fanciful solutions to very real problems. But his intrigues are doomed to failure. Euripides cannot free his father-in-law by inventing romantic escapes. He must deal openly with his enemies and make real concessions. The device by which he removes the Scythian comes not only from Old Comedy but also from his perception of the true nature of the virile policeman. Thus the comic view triumphs in the play because it deals honestly with the physical, spatial, sensible realities of man in his environment, whereas emasculated tragedy does not even take account of them.

How seriously should one take the criticism? The emasculation of tragedy, of course, suggests it has lost its vigor as well as its identity. If Agathon has no phallus and Euripides' devices fail, its art is effete. But does this have a political application? Perhaps tragedy, like a coward, has turned away from public problems or serious questions. It is true that the same Euripides who had earlier used the myths of the Trojan War to criticize Athenian imperialism (cf. *Trojan Women,* in 415 B.C.) was now writing romantic tragicomedies like *Helen.* Perhaps Aristophanes is also commenting ironically on his own emasculation. For instead of facing the questions of government, he is doing exactly what he blames

Euripides for. He has staged a play about a private quarrel between Euripides and his enemy, has made women or pseudowomen his characters, and the reality he faces is the body rather than the body politic.

Or is Aristophanes using the emasculation of tragedy as a latent metaphor for the political situation in 411? If tragedy has become effete, solving trivial problems with ingenious intrigues instead of heroically confronting real questions, perhaps the comedy implies that politics too has lost contact with truth and courage. For the politicians, like the poets, appear to resemble the playgirls at the Thesmophoria. Throughout the festival, women conduct their business by imitating the rituals and procedures of men in the assemblies. After juxtaposing public traitors and private enemies in their ceremonial curses, the women treat the subject of politics openly in the parabasis. But when these women compare themselves to their leaders, they offer no moral standard against which we can measure the corruption of the men; nor are there any common bonds to unite the sexes in peace and joy as in *Lysistrata*. Rather, the women, whose arguments belittle both themselves and the leaders of the government, symbolize perfectly the degradation of public life.

If the metaphor of emasculation applies to politics as well as poetry, *Thesmophoriazousai* may be a veiled comment on the shameless conspiracy of 411 and the citizens' cowardly reaction to it. We cannot bring Aristophanes back from Elysium to confirm this interpretation. We can only say that six years later in *Frogs*, Aristophanes used the state of the drama as an explicit metaphor for the state of Athens.

CHAPTER 8

Poets and Purgatory:
Frogs (Batrakhoi)

I Summary

A T the Lenaean festival of 405 Aristophanes submitted the the *Frogs*. Not only did the play win first prize, but it was performed a second time because the citizens were so impressed by the serious advice offered in the parabasis.[1] Athens had suffered a great deal in the six years that separate *Frogs* from *Thesmophoriazousai*. The old democracy had been overthrown by the oligarchic Council of Four Hundred which was firmly established in the summer of 411 through a conspiracy and a campaign of terror. Only four and one half months later they too were replaced, this time by the rule of the Five Thousand, a combination of oligarchy and democracy, with full civil rights granted only to the wealthy. But it too lasted no more than a few months. By 410, the extreme democracy had regained full power under the rule of the violent and self-serving demagogue Cleophon.

In this period of internal turmoil, the empire moved dangerously close to dissolution. Alcibiades, however, hoping to return home, helped defeat Athens' enemies in a brilliant series of victories (410, 408, 407) which nearly reestablished her power. But scarcely had he been recalled and made general, when he was exiled again. This time he withdrew from politics, leaving Athens to less astute leaders. Although the Athenians had just scored a naval victory at Arginusae in the summer of 406 and the Spartans were offering peace proposals, Cleophon boldly rejected their overtures. The ten victorious generals, however, were condemned illegally en masse for failing to rescue their dead at Arginusae. Six of them were actually executed while the fleet lay idle, and Sparta took the opportunity to rearm. Six months after the presentation of *Frogs* at the

Lenaea, Athens was finally defeated in the battle of Aegospotami and forced to give up her remaining possessions, tear down her walls, and submit to a government imposed by Sparta.

The same poet who watched Athens plunge toward inevitable defeat also witnessed a sharp decline in the fortunes of his own profession. In 407 Euripides died far away from home in Macedonia. By 406, after leading a public dirge to his rival, Sophocles too was dead at the age of ninety. Agathon had already left the city to continue his career in the court of King Archelaus of Macedonia. The absence of men who no doubt provided friendship as well as aesthetic pleasure caused more than a sense of personal loss. To the discerning comedian, no great talent remained to continue the glorious tradition. The great dramas of the fifth century belonged to all the citizens, who paid the expenses, participated in the productions, and watched them as part of a public festival that celebrated the city as well as the gods. Indeed, the festival of Dionysus contains within itself the highest potential and the greatest achievements of Athenian democracy. In the *Frogs*, Aristophanes returned to the subject of *Thesmophoriazousai*, the state of contemporary drama. This time, however, the connection between drama and Athens is made explicit, and the death and rebirth of tragedy promise the immortality of the state.

The comedy begins when Dionysus, the god of tragedy, enters the orchestra costumed in the boot and robe of tragedy as well as the lionskin and club of Heracles. He leads a donkey who bears his slave who in turn bears a huge basket of Dionysus' possessions. They are on their way to Heracles' house to ask for an itinerary of Hades, since Heracles has already been there. Dionysus wants to go down to the underworld to bring Euripides back from the dead so he can enjoy good tragedy once again. After Heracles describes the journey, the two go on their way, meeting first a corpse and then Charon, the mythological figure who ferries the dead across the Styx. Xanthias the slave must run around the shore, but Dionysus can climb aboard if he is willing to row. A chorus of frogs sings the parodus song which sets the rhythm for rowing. Once reunited on the other side, Dionysus and Xanthias move hesitantly through the chamber of horrors until they meet a new group, the chorus of initiates into the Eleusinian Mysteries, who sing a far more elegant lyric in celebration of their rules and deities while their leader, in anapests associated with the parabasis, solemnly forbids participation by enemies of the gods, the state, and good poetry. Dionysus and Xanthias proceed toward Pluto's palace, directed by the chorus, but their progress is interrupted by various inhabitants who mistake Dionysus for Heracles. Since that noble hero left behind a trail of unpaid bills and overeager mistresses, Dionysus is hounded by avengers and benefactors in turn. He keeps exchanging disguises with Xanthias so that he can enjoy the windfalls while his slave suffers the blows. But his cleverness ends in a beating for both before Aeacus takes them to Pluto to determine their true identities. While the actors are inside, the chorus of initiates drops its dramatic character to deliver the rest of the parabasis, lampooning leaders and offering practical advice.

Then Aeacus and Xanthias emerge to discuss the events within. Their conversation, like a second prologue, explains the situation. Euripides has challenged Aeschylus' right to public honor as the best tragedian and Dionysus has arrived just in time to judge the contest between them. The three characters come out and take their places for the agon. The formal debate develops from shouting and near blows into an organized presentation of charges and countercharges about literary devices, effect on the audience, and political programs. Dionysus has a hard time making up his mind, but, at the end, to Euripides' hurt surprise, he gives in to his *psyche* (heart and soul) and chooses Aeschylus. Pluto leads everyone to a feast and sends Aeschylus and the visitors off with advice, good wishes, and songs by the initiates.

II   Old Comedy and the Athenian Dionysus

The prologue begins in the same way as *Birds* or *Thesmophoriazousai*. Two characters enter from the parodus looking for somebody. Their dialogue both warms up the audience and provides the necessary information. The identities of Dionysus, god of the festival, and his slave are revealed by their words as well as their dress, for their subject is the art of comedy, or, as Richmond Lattimore translates Xanthias' opening question, "Should I give them any of the usual jokes, master? / You know the ones that are always good for a laugh." The characters' obvious awareness of the spectators as well as Dionysus' reference to his statue in the front row (l.16) warn the audience that they are watching a performance designed to affect them in a certain way. This introduction is very important to the plot and theme of the whole play. Dionysus' response begins an extended criticism of the devices of comedy, all the funnier in context because he and his slave use the very jokes they profess to condemn. The humor evoked by the incongruous sight of Xanthias bent under burdens while he rides the donkey is enhanced by their discussion of slapstick, farce, obscenity, and scatology which emphasize his discomfort. They too will indulge in these low devices as they progress though Hades, alternately bold or lascivious and defecating in fear, to the riotous scene where they try to stifle their cries as Aeacus beats them.

Comedy's unique reduction of the pompous, the powerful, and the perilous is also obvious, if unanalyzed by the characters. Pointed lampoons of bad poets and worse politicians ridicule their faults and failures and thus destroy their threat to the individual. Heracles, the tragic hero par excellence who is deified in myth because of his capacity for suffering, appears in this comedy, as well as in the *Birds*, as the great womanizer and glutton, the man who has drunk the full cup of life with impunity. When Dionysus compares his need for Euripides to Heracles' longing for pea soup, he trivializes and therefore dispels the seriousness of human pain. The attack on Dionysus disguised as Heracles emphasizes that Heracles has gotten off scot-free, providing a wish fulfillment for those in the audience who fear the very real consequences of acting out their own urges. The ridiculous figure of Dionysus himself, intimidated and out-shone by his slave, mocked by Heracles for his costume, and finally beaten by Aeacus, reduces the gods themselves and the impenetrable cosmos to human and controllable dimensions.

And if the deepest fear in the human psyche is the fear of death, this comedy breaks through the limitations of mortality. Heracles' return from Hades conveys the possibility of triumph over death. Dionysus dismisses the ways to get there—by choking, poison, and plunging from the rocks—as temporary discomforts rather than gruesome finalities. Existence in the underworld, from Heracles' itinerary and Dionysus' experience, appears as not so different from life on earth, full of people and places, some pleasurable and some not. Thus death becomes simply another form of life. The corpse Dionysus and Xanthias meet on the way retains the power to assert his indominable will; he prefers death to work! Of course, when the travelers reach their goal and enjoy the company of the blessed, life in the underworld, or death, has lost many of its terrifying aspects. Instead it contains beauty and joy for eternity.

Frogs is the only extant play of Aristophanes in which the fantasy is conceived and carried out by a god and his slave rather than by a representative of the Athenian populace. Several factors related to the change in community life must have prompted this artistic decision. In the first place, it is clear that the god of the dramatic festival could represent the city and its grandeur in a way that another Demos or Dicaeopolis could no longer, since the citizens were too divided and powerless in 405 to accept ridicule. Whereas Aristophanes had only implied an analogy between drama and government in *Thesmophoriazousai* in 411, by 405 the parallel was obvious.

The descent into Hades is, of course, a standard myth pattern, going as far back as the *Odyssey* in Greek literature. Before he can achieve his goal, the hero is forced to confront death, or his own limitations, isolation, and individuality. Heracles was sent to Hades to bring back Cerberus, the three-headed dog who guards its entrance, whereas Dionysus himself, in myth, descended to redeem his mother Semele and bring her to Olympus. The mission to rescue someone from the dead was also a common plot device in comedy.[2] But the choice of Dionysus as the central quester of the *Frogs* permits the analogy between art and politics to develop on a grand scale and to include comedy as well as tragedy and past as well as present. If Dionysus himself is a buffoon through most of the play, his myths recount the ultimate triumph of life in its eternal struggle with death, and he is still Athens deified, immortalized, and thus rendered timeless.

In the *Frogs*, the worship of Dionysus is also related to Demeter and the Eleusinian Mysteries, a cycle of public festivals, unique to Athens, in which citizens and foreigners, women and slaves, were offered the opportunity to become initiates into a cult which promised a blessed afterlife.[3] In myth, both Dionysus and Heracles became initiates before going down to Hades. Thus, their descent and return reassures the spectator-initiates that rebirth inevitably follows death. In Athens as well as in the world of *Frogs*, Dionysus, the god of tragedy, is also Iacchus, the god of the mysteries. It is he who leads the sacred procession from Athens to Demeter's shrine at Eleusis where many of the rites were celebrated. These ceremonies had been curtailed since 413, however, because of the enemy occupation of Attica. Only in 408, when Alcibiades escorted the procession to Eleusis with an armed guard, were the initiates able to celebrate the festival completely. Thus, like tragedy, the Eleusinian Mysteries represent both the greatness of Athens and its present problems.

But Dionysus does not go alone. He is accompanied by his slave. Xanthias is, on one level, the comic figure who punctures the pretensions of his superiors by his own earthy comments and acts. Since *Frog's* criticism of the art of comedy is incomplete without the elements of humor introduced by this figure from low life, Xanthias is the necessary companion to the divine hero. His presence also allows the common man in the audience to identify with the success of the fantasy. He is as much a hero as Trygaeus or Dicaeopolis, as clever as his divine master and twice as brave. So clever is he that the identities of the two questers become confused and inseparable just before they reach their goal. The hilarious reversal of roles masks a serious question. Is this a ritual imitation of chaos before creation, when all the rules of order are turned upside down, as in the Roman Saturnalia? Or is it in part a dramatic representation of Athens' and drama's own loss of self and sense of purpose in the last years of the war?[4]

Xanthias is long forgotten by the end of the play. The arrogant slave belongs to comedy rather than the more noble world of tragedy that is criticized in the contest of the two poets. But his presence in the first half provides a catalyst for two related elements of Old Comedy. Dionysus the god lives outside time, whereas comedy feeds upon the temporal and the topical. Xanthias is the link to daily life in Athens—its kitchen-eyed view of the city with its trivial business, disappointments, bread and circuses, and its backstairs revenge on the mighty. His status as slave makes possible numerous allusions to important contemporary events, like the naval battle at Arginusae in which slaves were allowed to fight for the first time and were given their freedom after the victory. There are also references to the demagogues who initiated the trial of the generals after the victory. Xanthias, comedy's eternal survivor, did not participate in the battle of "the cold meat" (or corpses, l. 191). His regrets and excuses, however, reassure the citizens of the bravery of their sailors and the wisdom of granting them citizenship. This is precisely the point that the chorus picks up in the parabasis. Even Dionysus will become a rower like those at Arginusae as he makes his descent into the underworld. Thus, the timeless and the temporal are blended as Xanthias and the god journey together toward the Land of the Blessed.

To get there, they must cross the River Styx. Charon, the aged boatman, ferries free men across, charging, not the mythical fee but two obols, the price of the theater ticket and the amount of the war-

time citizens' doles reinstituted by Cleophon.[5] This brief reference
again allows the audience to participate in the journey. While
Xanthias is forced to walk around the shore, Dionysus must take his
place at the bench like a common rower. Of course, the god has no
experience as a seaman, but Charon says that music will help him
learn the rhythmic movements. The singers are introduced as Swan-
Frogs, a name which connects them with death, since Swans were
believed to sing only at their last hour. Their song, however, reveals
their intimate connection with Dionysus and the marshes sacred to
him. This is somewhat ironic in the context. Their lyrics, which imitate the beat of Athenian rowers, are simply too fast and elaborate
for him. He sings an angry duet with them in lyrics which attempt
to slow them down. In the course of the song, two things happen.
First of all, he is clearly humanized by the activity. He ends up with
blisters on his bottom and the same aches and bruises that Xanthias
complained of when the prologue began. Secondly, he has become
an Athenian, an experienced rower. By the time he has reached the
other side of the Styx, he has learned to row so fast and sing so loudly that he reduces the frogs to silence. Thus the disguised Dionysus
has put on a new identity. He is the Athenian hero, that comic
blend of cowardice and bravery, driven by instincts toward freedom
and pleasure. These new temporal and mortal characteristics make
him almost indistinguishable from Xanthias.

The scene between Dionysus and the frogs is very important to
the abstract of comedy that the first part of the play presents.[6] The
god of comedy confronts the old animal chorus from the comos,
familiar from *Birds* and *Wasps*. Like some other comic choruses
they are hostile to the hero. The duet, in effect, is a telescoped comic parodus in which Dionysus, like Dicaeopolis or Pisthetaerus,
triumphs over the opposition. The chorus' words clearly connect
them to vitality and life in nature. Moreover, the frogs' music,
associated with Pan's reed as well as Apollo's lyre, reflects the noise
and activity of daily life, reminding the audience of rowing and
blisters as well as marshes and croaks. The Dionysus they sing is the
god of the Pot Feast and drunken revels, connected specifically with
low life and with Athens. Their introduction as Swan-Frogs,
however, underlines the intimate connection between life and
death, or comedy and tragedy.

The second chorus provides a marked contrast with the first. The
sound of flutes and the smell of torches warn Dionysus and Xanthias
that a sacred procession is approaching. Solemn and reverent for the

first time, they sit down quietly to watch the entrance of a chorus of white-robed men and women who have been initiated into the mysteries. The parodus song begins with a call to Dionysus to come and lead their dance. This time, however, he is called Iacchus, companion to Demeter and Persephone and leader of the procession to Eleusis where the goddess first established the mysteries. He is associated not with the noise and bubbling waters of the marshes, but with the bright purifying firelight and the deep-flowering meadows of the Land of the Blessed. The dance will be merry and the songs full of jokes and jibes, but the emphasis is clearly on the perfect and eternal. The light Iacchus brings rejuvenates the knees of the old men so that they shake off the pains of time's cycle of years (ll. 345 - 47).

The parodus continues as an elaborate series of lyrics, punctuated by instructions from the chorus leader and duets between Dionysus and Xanthias. First the chorus warns away the profane, juxtaposing the enemies of good theater and good government, making explicit the analogy between poetry and politics. Next the chorus invokes Demeter and Persephone, summons Iacchus once more, and sings a series of lampoons before directing Dionysus to Pluto's palace and moving forward to their destination. The lyrics all imitate the structure, grammar, and vocabulary of cult songs while alluding to the famous sacred places along the route from Athens to Eleusis. But like the festivals of Dionysus, the festivals of Demeter contain both the serious and the funny (cf. ll. 389 - 90). The string of stanzas in which the chorus attacks demagogues and degenerates actually represents the old rustic lampoon at the bridge which was a special feature of the festivals.[7] Thus, the blending of solemn worship with joyful dance, light comic rhythms, and lampoons is not only appropriate to comedy, but also to the Eleusinian Mysteries. Through the imitation of public ceremonies, allusions to Athenian sites, and satire of citizens, the parodus effectively brings the imagery of art, eternal life, and the Athenian state together.

Here, as in the song of the frog chorus, the god Dionysus, unseen by the worshippers, is watching the worship of himself. This irony adds a further dimension to the identification between the questers and the city. For Dionysus and Xanthias join in the dance, becoming, in effect, initiates themselves. On one level, this dramatizes the eternal truth of myth and ritual, for Dionysus the god always leads the procession and is ever an initiate, having undergone the ceremony himself before going to Hades to rescue Semele. But, on

another level, Dionysus, already aching and blistering from his stint
as Athenian sailor, now becomes further identified with mortals.
The chorus leaves him at the door to Pluto's house, where he meets
Aeacus and the friends and enemies of Heracles. The scene contains
all the elements that produce great comedy—farce, slapstick,
scatology, mistaken identity, reversals, exaggeration, debunking of
pretensions, and, of course, Aristophanic wit. But, as Whitman has
pointed out, the imagery in Hades all centers on shifting of identities or the lack of definition in the characters.[8] Dionysus has
already been terrified by the monster Empusa who has shifted from
bull to cow to girl to dog. As he and Xanthias continually change
disguises, the chorus encourages the slave to put on the boldness of
Heracles with his clothes. They compare Dionysus' self-serving
transformations to the methods of Theramenes, a naval captain at
Arginusae who was able to escape the wrath of the citizens by blaming the admirals for the failure to rescue the dead. The central question of the scene develops from "Who is Heracles?" to "Who is the
real god?" Until Pluto can answer, Dionysus has lost his divinity.
He and the city and the politics he has been associated with are, in
effect, dead and in hell. Athens has already been placed there
metaphorically at the beginning of the play when Dionysus assures
Heracles that if Sophocles was content in Athens, he will be content
in Hades (l. 82). Since the actual initiation into the Eleusinian cult
was a secret, Aristophanes dramatizes instead the physical and psychological journey toward death. By the logic of the mysteries,
however, rebirth into eternity will inevitably follow.

While Dionysus is in limbo, on the brink between life and death,
awaiting the verdict of Pluto, the chorus offers sound advice while
the city itself is on the brink, "tossed in the arms of the waves," (l.
704), but "still has time to change its way," (l. 734). They plead for
a pardon for those who associated themselves with the oligarchy so
that all brave citizens can fight together against the common
enemy. Like the characters, they allude to Arginusae, affirming the
wisdom of freeing slaves while stressing that their errant masters
should be granted the same generosity. As the characters within distinguish the false god from the real, the chorus advises the spectators to separate the good leaders from the bad, using an analogy
from minting that was especially topical since the coinage had just
been debased.[9] The ode and antode contain lampoons typical of the
parabasis. The chorus begins the opening ode by calling on the
Muses, patrons of human art, to join the holy songs and dances of

the blessed, but they move on to lampoon Cleophon as the demagogue who has faked his music as well as his citizenship. Their ridicule of Cleagenes, the bathman who cheats on the soap, picks up the imagery of the real and the false. Thus, in this parabasis, the chorus integrates its advice and comments with the action of the characters by means of references to events and imagery taken from the body of the play. And the chorus, which calls itself sacred (l. 680), is as much concerned with the citizens' future glory as with its own immediate survival. Thus the audience, alternately addressed as citizens wisest by nature and stupid fools, must feel itself also on the brink, without definition until the journey is completed by the return from Hades.

III *Tragedy—Old and New*

The play now splits in half, perhaps in imitation of the structural innovations Euripides introduced in tragedies like *Hippolytus* and *Mad Heracles*, but probably because the mythological underworld divides itself between the place of punishment and the Land of the Blessed. Xanthias' conversation with Aeacus, who is represented as the slave of Pluto instead of the mythical divine judge of the dead, functions as a second prologue which helps transport us from the temporal world of comedy to the timeless realm of tragedy. The former belongs to the slaves and sailors who relish dirty tricks and ridicule of their betters. Their triumph is assured; they even have their own Zeus to protect them. A noise from within disrupts the new camaraderie of Xanthias and Aeacus and prompts Aeacus to explain Euripides' challenge to Aeschylus. Now we enter the world of the masters which is supposed to be the arena for great affairs, noble men, and heroic gestures expounded in grandiloquent language. But something is clearly wrong. Euripides has initiated the challenge by playing to the groundlings and wooing them away from Aeschylus with cheap rhetorical tricks. Aeschylus, closely associated with goodness, refuses to allow Athenians to judge the contest. Sophocles will fight only if Aeschylus loses, and not for himself, but for the sake of art. Thus, tragedy, like the city and the god, is in limbo, in danger of losing its identity, with both poets and spectators contributing to its demise. The contest Aeacus describes is also a search for selfhood and merit in art, government, and the city.

The distortions, language, and allusions to daily life continue after the slaves withdraw, but the chorus' first song sets a new and elevated tone which develops within the comic framework. The initiates describe the imposing appearance of Aeschylus in an ode which resembles an Aeschylean parodus. It contains four consecutive strophes and employs the metrical usages, grammatical structure, and diction that Aeschylus used to create a sense of stateliness.[10] Euripides and Dionysus then emerge talking, but at first Aeschylus refuses to speak. His silence is a parody of his own use of a silent actor such as Cassandra or Pylades in the *Oresteia* to increase tension.

The preliminaries to the agon reveal the characteristics of the well-known participants. Although he remains indecisive and is sometimes silly, Dionysus, the comic quester, has become the god of tragedy, now speaking with authority and in a more dignified manner. Aristophanes has distorted the personalities of the two poets for the purposes of his comedy. The real Aeschylus was not a political reactionary nor did he avoid creating women characters, as the *Oresteia* makes quite clear. But he was long dead by the time Euripides and Aristophanes reached the height of their powers. Most of the audience probably never knew him. Therefore this remote poet, famous for fighting at Marathon (490 B.C.), could be used as a symbol of Athens' heroic past. Aeschylus' silence, poetic diction, and nobility reflect his distance from contemporary life. He is connected with mysterious nature instead, with the God of Storms, with light, and especially with Demeter to whom he addresses his simple prayer at the opening ceremony of the agon.[11]

In their ode the chorus introduces Euripides as "the man who works his mouth" (l. 826). He is, of course, the comic caricature of the tragedian, already familiar from *Acharnians* and *Thesmophoriazousai*. In *Frogs*, however, Aristophanes distorts two particular aspects of his art. First of all, he is the poet of daily life. His plays are filled with the language, people, and activities of the household and the marketplace. He has consciously removed the mystery so that men can comprehend and judge his art (ll. 959 - 61). He even treats the making and judging of poetry as if it were a trade like any other, with a tangible product that can be chopped like food or has parts to be measured out and put together like a wall. To him, the divinely inspired poet of old has become a mere artisan. This last point is related to his other outstanding aspect. He is, first and foremost, a man of his age, a product of the new philosophy which has placed its faith in human reason. Thus he reduces everything, poetry and speech, to scientific measurement and investigation. His analogies come from medicine and engineering, and his opening prayer is addressed to the new gods, Aether and Tongue on a Pivot, patrons of the noisy new art of rhetoric. His speech is sprinkled with allusions to contemporary Athenians such as Theramenes, and he refers to his gods as newly struck coins. These cross-references to earlier sections of the play connect Euripides to the temporal world of comedy and descent, or death, rather than with Demeter and eternal life.

Both playwrights take their art very seriously, however. Although they differ on techniques and subject matter, they accept the same criteria for judgment: the best poet is the one who is most skillful, offers intelligent advice, and makes men better. As Dover points out, Aristophanes does not discuss the ideas of *ate, hybris,* and *nemesis* (infatuation, pride, and divine revenge, respectively) or the value of moderation so important in tragic choruses, probably because these were unquestioned religious generalizations.[12] Instead his characters concentrate on the moral effect of their art on the audience. Here we have the antithesis already familiar from *Clouds.* The men of the Marathon generation gave the audience noble war heroes like Patrocles and thus fashioned brave patriots willing to risk everything, even life, for the state. But Euripides has presented suicidal adultresses, beggars, and, worse, constant talkers trained in rhetoric and philosophy. Therefore, the new man is either a degenerate, a coward and a shirker, or a thinker so filled with doubt that he is unable to act honorably. And form is meaning. Euripides boasts that he uses the language of men (l. 1058) to present his recognizable characters and comprehensible advice. But Aeschylus uses noble language to inspire men toward the fulfillment of their highest potential. The great ideas of heroic characters demand an eloquence worthy of them and capable of impressing and inspiring the spectators.

The second half of the play is a comic agon similar to the *Knights* in form. The contest is divided into several sections punctuated by odes in which the chorus comments on the progress of the debate. They open the proceedings with a prayer to the appropriate deities, the Muses, and at one point, assure the contestants that the audience can follow the technicalities of literary criticism. The dialogue is full of quotes misquoted or placed in an absurd context. Some lines consist of a ludicrous pastiche of memorable phrases whereas others are actually new verses written in the style of the

poet parodied.[13] Most of the features that are selected for distortion
are recognizable even to the casual reader of tragedy. The imagery,
blending the heroic with the banal, describes the debate as carpen-
try, a wrestling match, or a battle.

The contest begins with general discussion of obscure style versus
banality, of silence versus loquaciousness, of subject matter and of
effect. In the next bout, the poets examine each other's prologues.
Euripides picks apart Aeschylus' words to prove that they are both
redundant and meaningless, whereas Aeschylus can complete every
opening sentence Euripides offers with the phrase "lost his oil can."
The point of this interplay involves Euripides' monotony of structure and rhyme, his juxtaposing of the trivial and the grand, and,
possibly, his obscene innuendos. Euripides finally concedes defeat
and moves on to criticize Aeschylus' lyrics, charging him with
monotony too. Aeschylus retorts with a parody of a choral ode and a
monody which proves that Euripides gets his rhythms from vulgar
sources, lets his music control his words, and uses grand lyrics and
diction for the most trivial events and emotions. Aeschylus suggests
they use scales to measure the true weight of their poetry. This, of
course, is a parody of the famous scenes from epic (and Aeschylus'
lost play, *Psychostasia*) where Zeus measures the fates of heroes.
Aeschylus' martial lines outweigh Euripides' every time, for, as
Dionysus says, "Persuasion is a light thing" (l. 1396).

Still, Dionysus cannot decide. Each is his friend and a good poet.
Although he has come to Hades for Euripides, with not a thought of
Aeschylus, he has gained insight into himself and broadened his
perspective. When Pluto offers to let him leave with the poet he
chooses, Dionysus does not select Euripides immediately. Instead
he initiates one more contest, to see who can give the best advice to
the city. Although Euripides' counsel is couched in the pretentious
antitheses of the Sophists, it echoes the very words of the parabasis
of the chorus. Aeschylus suggests policies long outmoded, alluding
to the strategies of Pericles and even Themistocles. Dionysus finally
decides in favor of Aeschylus whom his *psyche* (soul), the immortal
seat of his feelings not his reason, desires. When Euripides protests,
Dionysus throws back at him two of his most famous lines ("My
tongue swore, not my mind" [*Hippolytus*, l. 612] and "What is
shameful, if those who do it do not think it shameful?", [fragment
from lost play *Aeolus*]), which are characteristic because of the
deceit and uncertainty they reflect. After the chorus sings a lampoon of Socrates, contrasting useless talk with true wisdom which

serves the state, Pluto sends Aeschylus and Dionysus back to life, urging that they send the demagogues quickly down to death and wishing happier days of light and joy to the city. Euripides is totally rejected; Sophocles must sit on the throne until Aeschylus returns. Dionysus, Art, and Athens have truly changed and become, in effect, immortal.

IV   *Aeschylus and the Eternal Athens*

Dionysus' choice of Aeschylus comes from his soul, from the life-giving and immortal spirit within and from the seat of his feelings. The elaborate test of skills has left him undecided about who is the better poet. There is no doubt, however, about whose is the better generation. Dionysus has, in fact, chosen the past over the present, a past that has already become mythic, so remote and grand that its representative, Aeschylus, is associated with light, fire, purity, and Demeter's Eleusinian Mysteries rather than the Athens that exists in time. In contrast, Euripides is the man of the present, of physical life and change. He is associated not only with innovative ideas about the gods, science, and rhetoric but also with the life of the body, with the tongue, the mouth, and immediate concerns of daily survival. He names his contemporaries in the manner characteristic of comedy and lampoon, whereas Aeschylus mentions or alludes only to dead heroes and patriots. Euripides' language is the language of the audience and his themes reflect their concerns. Even his advice is the only advice suitable for the moment at hand—the very counsel the chorus itself gives. Dionysus has apparently learned from his journey that the present city is not worth saving. The god who rushed down to Hades in quest of the poet with the freshest lines and the latest theatrical trick has changed so much that he prefers the oldest and most idealized in both art and politics.

Is this then a depressing comedy? Aristophanes makes obvious reference to what the audience must surely have admitted to itself by this time — that the city was rushing headlong to its final defeat. His attacks on leaders and policies are much more candid and urgent than in his earlier plays, for here they lack the juxtaposition with nonsense that usually renders the serious statement absurd. Moreover, he has directly attacked the city by comparing it with Hades and presenting the faults of the present generation, its selfishness, irresponsibility, cowardice, and devotion to useless pursuits. Clearly the city of 405, like the comic god, and recent tragedy, has lost its identity and merit.

Yet the framework of the mythic descent is one of hope — of the triumph of life over death, in which the defeat is necessary to the rebirth into eternity. And the entire play dramatizes the worthiness of the city per se, in its eternal aspects that should define it now and forever, even after the temporal defeat. For the small and the great, rower and poet, have earned the right to pass into the Land of the Blessed. The elements that are unique to Athens are exalted, through parody as well as praise, at the very moment that its present failures are condemned. The structure of the descent of Dionysus and his participation in the Eleusinian Mysteries are a grand eulogy to the public festivals the city offered its citizens and guests. The literary criticism of comedy and tragedy embodies a recognition of the immortality of art, as well as an appreciation of the city that supports it and a compliment to the audience clever enough to value and understand it. The audience is praised for its practical wisdom and heroism as well. Its reputation for these things will exist long after individual leaders and parties have made their own private descents. Six months before Aegospotami, the chorus and Euripides suggest that it may even be possible to avert disaster. But the whole tone of the play reassures us that if disaster is inevitable, so too is immortality. In choosing Aeschylus over Euripides, Dionysus is, in effect, celebrating the eternal Athens that cannot be hurt by this sad event. Thus, *Frogs* represents the essence of the spirit of comedy, for it dramatizes the ultimate wish fulfillment for city and individual alike — the triumph over death itself.

CHAPTER 9

New Comedy for Old: Ekklēsiazousai and Wealth (Ploutos)

I *Postwar Athens*

THERE is no precise information about Aristophanes' career in the interim between *Frogs* and *Ekklēsiazousai* (405 to ca. 392).[1] It is true that the destruction of the fleet at Aegospotami in 405 produced hard years for Athens. The Spartans captured the city, tore down its walls, and set up an oligarchy, the Rule of the Thirty, which governed through terror and in its own self-interest. The city was financially ruined and its citizens demoralized, but the energy and will of the Athenians were not so easily destroyed. By 404, led by Thrasybulus, they had expelled the Thirty, set up a moderate democracy, and proclaimed an amnesty so that oligarchs and democrats could work together to rebuild the state. The death of Socrates in 399 marked the new government's record with eternal and well-deserved infamy. The philosopher was probably a scapegoat for the community's hostility against his notorious pupils, Alcibiades and Critias, one of the Thirty tyrants. Aristophanes must have been horrified when his *Clouds* was used as evidence against Socrates. Plato, disillusioned by the government, left the city after the trial and rejected a career in politics.

By the middle of the decade, however, the city was clearly experiencing a recovery. It had participated in an alliance with its old enemies, Thebes, Corinth, and Argos, against the hegemony of Sparta. With the help of Persia its army had won a victory at Cnidus under the command of Conon. The city's fortifications were rebuilt and an economic revival was under way, due in part to the prospect of regaining an empire. (The fact that by 388, perhaps earlier, the number of comedies in the festivals was increased from three to five indicates that the city had returned to a peacetime budget.)

Problems remained of course: the widening gulf between the rich
and the poor, and the need to stimulate enthusiasm and faith in the
government. But once again Athens was a free and open society,
where a comedian could lampoon the plans and personalities of its
leaders.

II   Summary of Ekklēsiazousai

If *Ekklēsiazousai* reflects some of these problems, it is also a
testimonial to the rebirth of art and the state promised in the
Frogs. For the play contains many of the vigorous elements of Old
Comedy. It has a fantastic plot conceived and directed by a cunning
underdog. By the middle of the play, the action is accomplished,
and a series of episodic scenes then illustrates the effects of its
success. The familiar elements of Old Comedy's humor are present,
not only the vulgarities—sex, scatology, slapstick, and farce—but
also lampoons of particular individuals, institutions, and erudite
ideas, all couched in the ever-fresh Aristophanic wit. Yet subtle
differences in character, form, and tone foreshadow the decline of
Old Comedy and the transition to the less political Comedy of
Manners (called New Comedy) associated with Menander (342 -
290 B.C. in Athens) and his Roman imitators, Plautus and Terence
(254 - 184 B.C. and 195 - 159 B.C.).

Ekklēsiazousai (Women at the Assembly) resembles *Lysistrata*.
Again a female character conceives a grand scheme to solve Athens'
political difficulties. Praxagora (Busy in the Marketplace) and her
coconspirators disguise themselves as men and pack the assembly
(*ekklēsia*) so that they can vote themselves into absolute power. As
the play begins Praxagora waits impatiently outside her house for
the rest of the women who have agreed to meet before dawn. They
enter silently, without a lyric parodus, sporting body hair and
masculine clothing. Their inability to refrain from allusions to their
female lives humorously emphasizes the foibles of womankind as
well as the incongruity of the undertaking. But Praxagora's rehear-
sal speech ridicules the failures of male rule while proving the
superior character and business sense of Athens' wives and mothers.
Encouraged and defeminized, the chorus now marches off like
citizens racing to the assembly to get paid for their attendance.
While the women take over the meeting offstage, Praxagora's husband, Blepyrus, emerges from his house to defecate. Dressed in his
wife's shoes and cloak, his ludicrous appearance attracts the atten-

tion of his neighbor who also cannot find his clothes or his wife. Both men are in a hurry to get to the assembly. Blepyrus' problem is complicated by his painful constipation. Another citizen, Chremes, passes by and describes the unusual meeting. Some rascals have proposed foolish measures, and, unexpectedly, the assembly has voted to entrust women with the direction of the state. (Noting that the bill's supporters are pale and wan, he assumes they must be shoemakers who work indoors all day.) The men depart, dubious about this latest innovation in government, and disappointed at the loss of their salary. Then the chorus returns to Praxagora's house to remove disguises and slip home undetected. But as Praxagora is about to sneak inside, Blepyrus meets her and asks her where she has been and why she has taken his clothes. Satisfied by her lies, he describes the assembly. Although she feigns surprise, Praxagora proceeds to explain the women's platform to him—a communist state in which citizens will share land, food, riches, children, and sex partners. All will be so justly managed that there will be no work, no debts, no lawsuits, and no need for courtesans. After some objections, Blepyrus is won over completely. He is pleased to bask in his wife's glory as she organizes the first communal banquet.

The remainder of the play illustrates how the theory might operate in practice. In the first episode, one citizen prepares to turn all his property over to the state while his more materialistic neighbor withholds his own and mocks the other's idealism and credulity. When a herald announces the first common meal, however, the tightwad rushes in to get his share. The next episode examines the women's promise that everyone, even the oldest and the ugliest, will receive sexual satisfaction. An old woman and a beautiful girl sing a duet of insults as they prepare to receive a lover. The handsome young man who appears desires only the girl, but, according to the new law, he must first service the hag. As he tries to free himself from her embrace, he is accosted by a second older and uglier hag and then by a third, far worse than the other two. Protesting his fate, he is dragged off to bed. Meanwhile all the citizens have been eating and drinking together. In the finale, Blepyrus struggles in to dinner, leading several girls. After the chorus leader begs the audience to judge the comedy fairly, all dance gaily off to dinner while the servant describes the main dish, a gigantic word compounded of twenty-four kinds of food which Douglass Parker says "reproduces linguistically the hash it describes."[2]

III   *The Feminist Rebellion*

Although Praxagora's women defeat their men, the battle of the
sexes here lacks the bitterness of *Thesmophoriazousai* and the
violence of *Lysistrata*. Again the women are wives and mothers who
become more masculine as the action proceeds; they literally
transform themselves from giddy girls to irascible old assemblymen
before our eyes. In contrast, the men are emasculated by the reversal of political roles. Male citizens with androgynous characteristics
are lampooned in the prologue. The audience first sees Blepyrus as
a buffoon, dressed in his wife's clothes, and straining to give birth to
a bowel movement. When Praxagora begins to function efficiently
as the general he is happy to be the power behind the throne. But
there is no pejorative implication in his comic emasculation. The
success of the women's intrigue sounds even more impressive
because, ironically, a man describes their actions at the meeting
with approval, and the husband of the chief conspirator, unaware of
her imposture, agrees to all her arguments about the superiority of
women. It is clear that the men respect and value their women for
their ability to nurture families, manage households, and deal
honorably with other people.

Thus although the poet exploits the incongruity of women acting
like men and criticizes men by comparing the two sexes, he has not
chosen the battle itself as a metaphor for his social satire. Rather he
seems to have chosen women as main characters because they are
the most appropriate group to introduce the communist program
and to exploit its possibilities for pleasure. In fact, Dover suggests
that since Greek marriage was a means for transmitting property,
with the girl's father choosing the bridegroom for economic reasons,
"community of women and community of property were regarded
by the Greeks as cognate issues."[3] As citizens without property or
rights, they represent the political underdogs who would benefit
most by the change. Their domestic duties, however, make possible
the analogy between household management and government of
the polis. Ironically, this radical reform, as Praxagora implies, is
really just an extension of women's traditional method of sharing
the family's resources among its members equally. Most obvious, of
course, is the women's connection with sex and food. Thus their
own excesses, well-established in the prologue, permit the comic
distortion of the theory in practice and the exuberant Dionysiac
ending.

The prologue also establishes the superiority of Praxagora as the leader of the plot. Like other comic heroes, and Lysistrata in particular, she proves herself capable of conceiving and carrying out an intrigue against her rivals. Her ability to speak effectively, which makes her the equal of any male, is established at the very beginning when she eulogizes the lamp. Douglass Parker suggests that the audience might at first actually mistake her for a tragic heroine.[4] The other women are so amazed by the eloquence and persuasiveness of her practice speech that they compliment her profusely, and one even applauds her as a brilliant man (l. 204). She is as intelligent as she is articulate, for she can detect any slip in the women's imposture as well as explain and defend the communist state she will organize. Moreover, she makes clear that she will be strong enough to fend off insults or attacks from the assemblymen. Her leadership effectively transforms ladies into men marshalled for action. But she is also as cunning as any rogue in Old Comedy, able to silence her jealous husband with lies and half-truths. In the scene with Blepyrus, one gets glimpses of a female character type who might be the ancestress of Matrona, the wife of New Comedy who constantly harasses her helpless mate.

The women she leads are the comic chorus, but its role is considerably reduced. Instead of dancing and singing in a typical parodus, the women enter silently, one by one, or in small groups, as the dramatic situation demands, for they are sneaking away from home in the dark to rehearse the conspiracy. Their first lyric is actually an exodus, in which they leave the orchestra like assemblymen from the countryside complaining about city dwellers and regretting the good old days. They enter again after the meeting has been described by Chremes; now they sing of their anxiety as they hasten to remove their disguises and slip discreetly back into their domestic roles. After praising Praxagora as she outlines the new order, they take no further part in the drama. In the two places where one would expect a lyric to separate the episodes (ll. 729 and 876), the word *chorou* (of the Chorus) appears instead in the manuscripts. The chorus of assemblywomen, with its character tied to the plot, has completed its function as a participant in the action. The drama now illustrates the effects of their plot by means of two unrelated episodes in which the group of women play no part. It is possible that the word *chorou* was inserted in a later edition at the points where these later episodes end and the actors have left the stage, in imitation of the manuscripts of New Comedy.

If, however, *chorou* was part of the original text, one may see here in embryo New Comedy's use of choral lyrics as interludes between acts, unrelated to the plot at hand.[5] The chorus reappears at the end *qua* chorus, to appeal to the spectators for a favorable judgment of their play, in a manner reminiscent both of Old Comedy's parabasis and of the actor's plea for applause which usually concludes a New Comedy. In Bacchic ecstasy, they dance off the stage with the actors eagerly anticipating, according to Ussher, the free meal they will get from their sponsor if *Ekklēsiazousai* wins first prize.[6]

Praxagora and her women claim several times that they are acting as saviors of a troubled state, and the men repeat their criticisms of the government's leaders and the citizens in general. There is no attempt to refrain from lampoons of individuals or from attacks on specific actions and institutions. Many individuals are lampooned for their unusual physical characteristics such as hairiness, effeminacy, and bleary eyes. But the demagogue Agyrrhius receives most of the abuse, and for a serious reason. He instituted a salary for attendance at the ekklesia and then raised the fee to three obols a day to attract more citizens to public service. Although the need for such a proposal indicates the poverty that plagued the state, the women view the fee as a sad commentary on the mercenary qualities and lack of patriotism of contemporary citizens. Against the demagogue who proposed it, however, their judgment is more harsh. Agyrrhius has clearly purchased the votes of the citizens who depend on that fee for their livelihood. They imply that the salary has increased the gulf between the rich, who can afford to remain unbought, and the compromised poor. Moreover, it has even forced the rural assemblymen to race to the Pnyx before dawn to beat the urban citizens to the money. Aristophanes may have had a further reason for singling out Agyrrhius for ridicule since he, in an effort to economize, lowered the payment to the comic poets.[7] Chremes reports that another clever schemer, one naked Evaeon, has generously proposed for his own benefit that fullers give cloaks to all the poor and tanners provide beds in winter.[8] The popularity of such government giveaways, confirmed by Blepyrus, may have influenced Aristophanes' choice of the subject, for the women's communist state pushes the principle behind the dole to its logical and most extreme conclusion.

The citizens are ridiculed as much as the leaders who pander to their needs. The indecisiveness of the people is a prime target. Praxagora refers to recent alliances made and instantly regretted and leaders often used and then abused. Supporting her point, the citizens who discuss the merits of turning in their private property review a series of government economic decisions made and then swiftly reversed at the individual's expense. Worse, the citizens are frantic innovators: their society exhibits *polupragmosune* of *Birds* (cf. pp. 114 - 15) gone wild, seething with purposeless frenetic movement toward whatever is new. Praxagora praises women because they, in contrast, act always according to custom-law, sticking to proven ways. Ironically, her plan is accepted not because it seems conservative but because it has never been tried before.

IV *Utopia*

Although Praxagora introduces the program as a radical departure from custom, it would not have been entirely strange to the spectators. Herodotus describes similar societies such as the Agathysi who live together as a single family to avoid jealousy and hatred (*The Histories*, Bk. IV, Ch. CIV). And the Lycurgean constitution of Sparta resembles her plan. To the modern reader the parallels with Plato's views in the *Republic* are most striking. In both states, citizens share property and sex partners. Children belong to all in common, so that all citizens regard each other as members of the same family. Because everyone has what he wants, there are no debts, no thieves, and therefore no lawsuits. All live and eat together, and, of course, there is no discrimination against women. Explanations of the similarities are inconclusive. It is impossible to prove the relations between the poet and the philosopher and whether one borrowed from the other or if they took their ideas from a common source.[9] The parallel itself, taken with the lampoons of the extremist democracy, suggests that Aristophanes selected communist speculation for satire because it was topical.

Aristophanes' treatment of the theory, however, is quite unplatonic. He is less interested in serious criticism of the ideas than in their comic potential. Praxagora explains her utopia in a scene very similar to a comic agon in which the doubters are convinced by the debate. Blepyrus functions here as the familiar buffoon whose obscenities and anxieties ridicule both the erudite theory and the intellectual pretensions of its defenders. And Praxagora persuades her listeners by appealing not to the needs of their souls, but to the needs of their bodies—for idleness, luxury, and SEX, SEX, SEX. She assures them that troublesome democratic institutions will

wither away. The law courts, symbolic of limitations to their
freedom, will soon become banquet halls. The voting urns that
represent the exhausting and unrewarding duties of citizenship will
now be used for assigning dinner places. Reduction of pleasure will
be the only form of punishment in this almost perfect society.

Although the theory seems foolproof, the remaining scenes examine its operation in practice. The first episode concerns the most
radical feature: the demand that all individuals turn their private
property over to the state. One citizen willingly complies with the
law, gathering together his beloved possessions and lamenting their
loss while his neighbor carps at his stupidity and holds on to his own
goods. Their debate satirizes some things unique to
Athens—citizens like constipated Anthisthenes or the debauched
Callias, short-lived political decisions, new attitudes to the *nomos*
(custom-law), and the national greed, so endemic even the gods
have upturned palms. But the characters seem more like universal
types who can be named Good Citizen or Bad Citizen instead of
comic distortions of Athenians who populate other Old Comedies.
Douglass Parker calls one such citizen Pheidolus or Stingy, imitating the manner of New Comedy.[10] And their dialogue reveals
two very basic human traits: Chremes or Good Citizen will obey
authority automatically, without reflection. The success of the new
system depends on men with such strong loyalty and trust. In this
utopian comedy he is in the majority; his neighbors, abused by Bad
Citizen, turn in their property too and are rewarded with the first
banquet. But the episode also dramatizes the selfish and assertive
side of human nature, often the strongest feature of the hero of Old
Comedy. Bad Citizen abuses his opponents, rejects restraints, holds
on to what is his, and like most of us tries to get something for
nothing.

The bawdy episode which follows exploits Praxagora's promise to
provide equality of sexual opportunity, by forcing attractive citizens
to service the undesirables before enjoying each other. Although the
chorus has disappeared, the lyricism remains, as women sing out to
their anxiously awaited lovers or against each other, and the young
lovers sing a duet. The series of lyrics imitates the meters and
language of banquet songs, folk songs, love songs, and other popular forms, with tragic parodies interspersed to mock the intensity
of passion. The setting in which women show themselves to the
public, and the duet itself, reminiscent of serenades to loose
women, effectively dramatize the ladies' new freedom in a typically

comic way.[11] Now the state does not prevent them from being what all women desire to be—nymphomaniacs. Obscenities abound when the girl's beauty and innocence are contrasted with the hag's experience. The young man adds to the lewdness with his obvious erection and his frank judgments of used bodies. Allusions to pudenda, positions, and perversions are ubiquitous. Old Comedy's unembarrassed presentation of sex develops in tandem with the increase in the heroines' power. The scene, of course, begins as a simple seduction, but ends in a gang rape. Now that the women have become the sexual aggressors, the reversal of roles promised at the beginning of the play is complete. The political underdogs will literally be on top. But the victim is not only a male; he is a youth. And the nubile girl left quivering with desire is as much a victim as he is. For the victorious women represent not only their sex but their age group, the old impoverished and harassed assemblymen as well as the constipated husbands fearful of impotence. The triumph of the hags repeats Old Comedy's triumph over old age, with its inevitable loss of vigor, and reverses the natural as well as the sexual order.

The lovers themselves seem precursors of characters in New Comedy. Their distinguishing features are their youth and their sexuality, but they are prevented from consummating their desires by the jealousy and interference of the older generation. Typically in New Comedy, the characters or their slaves evolve elaborate intrigues to escape to freedom and happiness. Their defeat here is necessary to underline the comic victory, but the audience has already been assured that, despite the postponement, the youths will soon be free to enjoy each other too, in Praxagora's utopia.

The finale dramatizes the total success of the women's plan. The banquet has already begun. Blepyrus has had his young girls, and now the audience is invited to share the food and drink.[12] The chorus, after praising the spectators' wisdom and sense of humor, begs them to remember this, the first play, and judge it fairly. Thus the parabasis of the earlier plays, full of music, metaphor, lampoon, and advice, has been reduced to these nine lines. But the exodus has all the exuberance of any other Old Comedy. The servant announces the eighty-three syllable main dish (in a breathless lyric full of irregular resolutions), and, in a typical joke which mocks the hopes she has aroused, she takes back the invitation of the last line. (cf. *Lysistrata*, ll. 1063 - 71, 1208 ff.). Then everyone dances off to enjoy his fill, shouting a cry to Bacchus, the god of the festival.

Ekklēsiazousai has many elements that foreshadow a different kind of drama, but most startling is the change in tone. The sense of urgency has vanished from the comic confrontation. The sexes battle each other without rancor. The chorus rarely attacks either the actors or the audience. Although players often face the spectators to lampoon individuals, to include them in the criticism of citizens in general (ll. 436 - 40), or to invite them to the dinner, there is no sustained attempt to make them participants, as in *Birds* or *Peace*, or to involve them in the serious problems the play pretends to consider, as in *Wasps*. Indeed, although political problems are implicit in the poet's choice of the fantasy, and some even surface in the satire, the play itself lacks the bitterness and serious conflict which charge the atmosphere of many of the earlier plays. One may try to account for the difference by pointing to the poet's age (50?) or by suggesting that after the defeat neither he nor the citizens took themselves and their destiny so seriously. The gentle tone, with the resulting universality of character, however, makes one feel that *Ekklēsiazousai* could take place almost anywhere, not just in fifth-century Athens.

V   Wealth

Wealth, produced in 388, reflects the same public situation as *Ekklēsiazousai:* poverty and civic lassitude despite signs of an economic and military recovery. But its plot and characters indicate society's movement away from the city as the focal point of the individual's life. *Wealth* is essentially a private drama which concentrates on the family rather than the citizen. The hero's actions are independent of contemporary political institutions or even of the cultural ambience of Athens. His plan arises from his own faith and goodness which have so far isolated him and doomed him to failure. There is no emphasis on his triumphant assertion of his physical self, so typical of Old Comedy and its ceremonial release. Furthermore, his success does not lead to a selfish fulfillment of his individual desires. Instead, he shares his happiness and effects a moral conversion of society as a whole. Thus *Wealth* points forward to the fourth century when men identify their happiness with moral virtue rather than physical pleasure and to New Comedy whose interests and characters are universal rather than topical.

Wealth is a utopian folktale which develops from the age-old proverb that wealth must be blind since it attaches itself to the undeserving. When Chremylus, a virtuous old man, asks Apollo if his son must become a rogue to survive, the oracle commands him to follow the first person he sees upon leaving the temple and to take him home. The blind beggar that he and his slave Cario pursue turns out to be Ploutos, the personification of wealth. After Chremylus promises to restore Ploutos' sight, so that he can recognize the deserving, Cario summons his master's friends, the chorus of poor but honest farmers, to share the wealth. The action is delayed by a neighbor, Blepsidemus, who refuses to believe that Chremylus has gotten rich honestly or will willingly share his fortune. Next, a horrible hag who calls herself Poverty rushes in to prevent the cure, insisting that she is responsible for all the blessings of civilization. Chremylus easily defeats her in a standard agon. Then the three men lead Ploutos to the temple of Asclepius for healing while the chorus performs an interlude.

After Cario describes Ploutos' cure, the god is led to Chremylus' house, and the final episodes illustrate the utopian results of the scheme. A just man is rewarded with new comforts, and an informer is punished for his sins. Another choral interlude follows. Then an old woman comes to complain; because no one needs money anymore, she can no longer buy the affections of a young man. Next Hermes and a priest of Zeus concede honor to the new god who has replaced them. All march out in a sacred procession to install Ploutos in his new shrine. Chremylus' promise that the youth will make love to the old woman one last time is a faint reminder of the exuberant love-feasts that conclude the earlier comedies of Aristophanes.

Wealth exhibits the characteristic structure of Old Comedy (prologue, parodus, agon, episodes, exodus), but is very different from the other plays. The most obvious difference is the diminished role of the chorus. Although they sing a parodus and seem to remain in the orchestra throughout the rest of the drama, none of their other lyrics has been transmitted in the text. Instead the word *chorou* appears in most manuscripts in the places where the actors have exited and some sort of interlude seems necessary.[13] This poses the problems of what the interludes consisted of—whether they were compressed and simplified lyrics unrelated to the drama, or flute solos, or dancing by a small group—and why the chorus' importance has declined so drastically—whether because of economic restrictions or censorship. Evidence suggests that the changing role of the chorus was dictated not so much by the political situation as by the changing interests of the audience who, after all, judged the plays in open competition.[14] When the action focuses on private and domestic concerns, the chorus' traditional function of exploring topical public issues (particularly in the parabasis, but also in the lampoons which comprise the agon and other odes) no longer has a place in the comedy. The effect of the new subject on the one lyric which has come down to us is clear. When, in the parodus, the chorus hears the good news about Wealth, the poor old farmers do not sing about themselves and their situation. Rather they imitate a dithyramb by Philoxenus, a contemporary poet, to express their joy.[15] The lyric is unrelated to the plot or the chorus' character, but does reflect the Dionysiac elements of the comos through its form and subject matter.

The reduction of the chorus' role points forward toward New Comedy in two ways. In the first place, the episodes become longer and more important. This is already clear in *Wealth*, which, like most New Comedies, contains five scenes. In addition, the increased importance of the actors and their plot changes the relationship between the chorus and the audience. The formal direct address is, of course, gone altogether. There is still some breaking of the dramatic illusion to establish contact with the spectators, but it is done by the actors, as when Cario searches the audience to find a single just man for the blind Ploutos (l. 99) or when Chremylus' wife notices one Dexinicus getting ready to catch the figs he expects the actors to scatter (ll. 800 - 801). But a new twist in the relations with the audience appears in two episodes. Both Blepsidemus and Chremylus speak apart to themselves (and to the audience) to mock their interlocutors, Chremylus and the old woman respectively, using the convention known as the aside, which becomes so important an element of New Comedy. Thus the audience now identifies with the actor's private drama instead of being forced, *qua* citizens, to take sides on public issues by the chorus' topical addresses.

The kinds of characters which populate this drama are also different: clear universal types rather than comic distortions of typical Athenian citizens. Chremylus himself is the best example, for, although he is old, poor, and clever, he lacks the roguishness and idiosyncrasy of a comic caricature like Dicaeopolis or Philocleon. Instead he is the upright family man who always acts reasonably and performs all duties correctly. Opposed to him is Blepsidemus, the skeptic. Two types of women also appear. The strong capable wife, who completes the family in this domestic drama, is similar to Matrona of New Comedy. The deluded old hag is obsessed with sex but her passion remains controlled and never breaches the limits of decorum. Other characters, the just man, the youth, even the informer, are exactly what their names imply with no unexpected or inconsistent characteristics. The use of such generalized characters precludes the raucous vulgar humor which results from extreme behavior and indecent wit. No poor man in *Wealth* is capable of selling his daughters as vagina / piglets like the starving Megarian in *Acharnians*.

Cario, the most interesting character, is both the descendant of Xanthias, Dionysus' slave in the *Frogs*, and the ancestor of all the crafty servants who manipulate the plots of New Comedy. He is an equal partner with Chremylus, sharing in the persuasion of Ploutos, announcing the god's cure, and even demonstrating the success of the plan by controlling the scenes in which the just man, the informer, and later Hermes come to Ploutos' shrine. In the prologue, he bewails his undeserved status as a slave. Despite threats of beatings and prison, he behaves boldly before his master, Ploutos, the chorus, Chremylus' wife, and the informer. But, instead of being punished for his impudence, he is rewarded with a share of all the new luxuries of his master's household. The slave's successful self-assertion is connected to the Saturnalian quality of the Dionysiac festival, in which the oppressed temporarily triumph over their oppressors. Dover speculates on the reason for the increasing importance of the tough and resourceful slave:

It is a fact, however, that fourth century comedy was progressively "softened" by reduction of the elements of violence, vulgarity and sexuality in the characters to whose happiness and success the plot leads, and in so far as elements of this kind were still welcome in comedy it was natural to transfer them, in the form of earthy cunning, self-regarding roguishness, to slave characters.[16]

Wealth attacks the same targets as the other Old Comedies, but it uses the satire differently. Most obvious is the ridicule of Olympian religion. Cario's opening speech censures Apollo for his insane oracle while Ploutos blames Zeus for blinding him and thus causing all the injustice in the cosmos. The report of the events in the temple makes fun of the rites of Asclepius by concentrating on the appetites and farts of the suppliants and by describing the priest's thievery. Here, as in *Peace*, Hermes is portrayed as a trivial divinity whose gluttony makes him easy to bribe. This ridicule reflects the sacred release implicit in comedy where, within the ceremonial worship, the Olympians, who are representations of cosmic necessity and are responsible for the patent injustices of human life, are reduced to comprehensible and therefore controllable dimensions. In *Wealth*, however, the comic hero does not triumph over the gods. Instead, ironically, Apollo's oracle is vindicated, and the earthly utopia is duplicated in the cosmos when Zeus reconciles himself to Ploutos.

The parody of tragedy provides another important element of the satire. As always, the devices which intensify the pathos of a tragic experience are parodied by comic characters in ludicrous situations. Cario begins by lamenting his fate in typical tragic style. He appears later like a tragic messenger to describe the healing of the blind god. The prologue introduces a plot similar to Euripides' *Ion* where another father is directed to follow the first person he sees upon leaving the temple and where Apollo's reason and morality are also open to question.[17] The scene in which Ploutos is forced to admit his identity is reminiscent of several tragic recognition scenes which effect significant reversals of the characters' situations. The opposition of sight and blindness, with its metaphorical implications about morality and wisdom, builds upon the ideas associated with those ubiquitous tragic characters, Oedipus and Tiresias. Hermes' entry, full of threat and bluster, imitates the ending of Aeschylus' *Prometheus Bound* when he comes as a messenger of his hostile master. Here his defection prefigures the reconciliation of Zeus. But in *Wealth* tragic allusions are presented without ridicule, perhaps to give spectators pleasure in their own powers of recognition or to add stature to the play's theme and comic reversal.

Wealth also contains some lampoon and political satire, but they are presented to develop the theme rather than for their own sake. When Chremylus and Cario enumerate all the people whose lives depend on money, their lampoons are closer to name-dropping than invective. More bitterness is directed against Neoclides, the notoriously poor-sighted politician (cf. *Ekklēsiazousai*, ll. 254, 398 ff.) who is accused of robbing the citizens blind.[18] Cario describes how Asclepius doctors him into excruciating pain and incurable blindness in order to prevent him from further perjuring himself. Thus the choice of Neoclides as a target emphasizes the poetic justice of the whole plot, for the blinding of the charlatan is balanced by the restoration of Ploutos' sight. The informer who appears at the end is treated even more harshly. But he is not an individual citizen. Rather he is a nameless type whose sins against the court system are clearly explained without comic distortion, and then emphatically condemned. Again his punishment demonstrates poetic justice. After falsely accusing the just man of stealing a new cloak, he is forced to give up his own to Ploutos and to take the just man's rags and warming place at the baths.

Dover uses the word "softened" to describe the new tone of fourth-century comedy, and there is no doubt that the comic vision of human life is "softer" in *Wealth*. The characters are no longer vulgar, self-seeking individuals whose success isolates them from their group. Rather their very reason and benevolence direct them toward a heroic quest which improves and unites society. (Only *Peace* is similar in this respect.) The exuberant obscenities, which glorify man's animal nature, and the vigorous displays of public controversy, which emphasize differences among men, have been replaced by the gentle portrayal of universal types who despite the fantasy of the plot behave realistically. The comic triumph over the forces of death is still present, of course, but it involves a much greater idealization of human existence, for man appears to be reasonable, and his society perfectible, and the cosmos is ultimately not hostile to his *summum bonum*. One can see in *Wealth* a movement away from the fierce individualism that characterized the last decades of the fifth century and an evolution toward the age of philosophy which really began with Plato.

CHAPTER 10

Conclusion

I Decline

OLD Comedy was nurtured by the community life of Athens.
Not only did the citizens support and participate in the
performances but they themselves often served as the main targets
of the satire. The poet ridiculed all of their cherished institutions—the family, the state, even the gods. Moreover, he exposed their cowardice, indecency, and hypocrisy. But contemporary
audiences never considered Aristophanes malicious or vulgar. And
the important citizens he lampooned laughed with the rest. This absolute freedom offered the community as a whole the opportunity
to purge the hostility to authority that may exist in even the most
democratic society. In addition, the individual citizen could over-
come his own sense of inadequacy and identify with divine Nature,
that great leveler whose cyclic order survives all catastrophes.

Yet comedy was changing, even in Aristophanes' lifetime. One
can detect new attitudes and artistic devices in his last comedies
which indicate that the audience's taste had changed. The
characters seem less particular, their actions less fantastic, and their
language less coarse. Moreover, there are fewer topical allusions.
However, the development toward New Comedy, the ancient
Comedy of Manners best exemplified by the plays of Menander,
was gradual. Some scholars have even posited a transitional form,
Middle Comedy, to account for the period between Aristophanes'
last play (388) and Menander's first (320).[1]

But the lives of Menander and his Athenian audience were so
different from Aristophanes' that historians have given the age a
different name—the Hellenistic Period—to distinguish the world of
the great empires of Alexander and his successors from that of the
fifth-century city-states. This new Hellenistic audience preferred

146

Menander. The Alexandrian critic of the third century B.C., Aristophanes of Byzantium, expressed the great appeal of the Comedy of Manners: "Menander and Life! Which of you imitated the other?"[2] In the second century A.D., Plutarch compared the two poets:

Coarseness in words, vulgarity and ribaldry are present in Aristophanes, but not at all in Menander; obviously, for the uneducated, ordinary person is captivated by what the former says, but the educated man will be displeased. . . . Morever, in his (Aristophanes') diction there are tragic, comic, pompous and prosaic elements, obscurity, vagueness, dignity, and elevation, loquacity and sickening nonsense. And with all these differences and dissimilarities, his use of words does not give to each kind its fitting and appropriate use.

Menander, in contrast, used polished and familiar diction appropriate to each character type. By judging according to the criteria of verisimilitude and propriety, Plutarch rejected the qualities which distinguish Old Comedy. Plutarch's metaphor sums up the attitude: Aristophanes' poetry is "Like a harlot who has passed her prime and then takes up the role of a wife whose presumption the many cannot endure and whose licentiousness and malice the dignified abominate."[3]

Fortunately, scholars never neglected Aristophanes, even when they did not appreciate his poetry. The texts of his comedies were copied, studied, and interpreted, beginning in the third century B.C. at the Library at Alexandria. Aristophanes was especially valued as a primary source by the grammarians of the Roman Empire who were trying to imitate pure Attic Greek. The Byzantine scholars of the ninth century produced the manuscripts on which our own editions are based. They used wide margins, so that they could include with the text the exegesis which had been accumulating since the Alexandrian period. These scholia provide information on vocabulary, production, and political allusions. Modern classicists have not only established reliable texts but have also rejected the criteria of verisimilitude and propriety. The discovery of the relation between comedy and fertility ritual (whatever it may have been precisely) has led back to a genuine appreciation of the fantasy and free form, as well as the "presumption . . . licentiousness and malice" of Old Comedy.[4]

II *Rebirth*

By now dramatists as well as scholars have rediscovered Aristophanes and have responded with enthusiasm, recognizing that he has much to say to a twentieth-century audience. We, like the Athenian citizens of his generation, take pride in our democracy and our position of world leadership. Yet after world wars and cold war confrontations, we have begun to lose confidence in our own myths and idealism. So we easily comprehend a satirist who exposes the failures of big government and its leaders. America too has its *Knights* out of *Oedipus Rex:* Barbara Garson's *MacBird,* a bitter reaction to President Kennedy's assassination based on Shakespeare's *Macbeth.* Yet the very fact that we are free to criticize confirms for us, as it did for them, the value of our imperfect system.

Like the Athenians, we have founded our society on principles of equality and individualism. Aristophanes' basic fantasy of the common hero who triumphs by his native wit corresponds to our own concept of the self-made man. So too does his exposé of the affectations of the intellectual elite have parallels in our democratic art. Moreover, the fantasy offers us the same wish fulfillment it offered his troubled audience. We have become conscious of our inability to solve all the problems of our increasingly complex society. But, for the moment at least, Aristophanes makes everything, from overnight success to world peace, possible.

Aristophanes speaks to his audience in a particularly modern way. Our age, reacting to the excesses of Victorian prudery, is one of the few in which sexual frankness has been permitted and even exalted in art. Happily, *Lysistrata* can now be translated without circumlocution and produced in authentic costume, complete with erect phalluses, to be fully appreciated by the unblushing granddaughters of men who were not even allowed to read the play in Greek.

Old Comedy's mixture of reality and illusion, with its disjunctive structure, corresponds to certain tendencies in modern art, music, and poetry. In revolt against the rationalism that has led us to the brink of atomic war, we too make war on the canons of art. Free verse, by its very name, proclaims its liberation from the restraints of traditional forms, while the paintings of Picasso distort and fragment reality, and the music of John Cage makes concerts out of random audience noise. Like Aristophanes, we use our art forms to mock our myths and even to devalue art itself. Mel Brooks' movies, *Blazing Saddles* and *Young Frankenstein*, ridicule western and horror films, just as Aristophanes ridicules tragedy in *Frogs*. Yet, by juxtaposing reality and fantasy, the ancient and modern comedians expose the grandeur as well as the failures of their societies' dreams.

Aristophanes speaks directly to us through such topical themes as the battle of the sexes, the scandals of power politics, and the underdog's need to strike back at his oppressors. Sometimes this relevance results in a misunderstanding of his original intention. *Acharnians* has been read as pacifist propaganda, whereas *Lysistrata* and *Ekklēsiazousai* have become feminist documents instead of the comic fantasies they really were. However, as demonstrated by a recent production of *Lysistrata*, in which the Spartans were played by blacks in tribal dress, Aristophanes remains perennially fresh and adaptable.

Notes and References

Chapter One

1. From *Life 9,* one of several ancient biographies which provide little accurate information. See Pauly-Wissova et al., *Reäl Encyclopadie der classischen Altertumswissenschaft* (Stuttgart: Metzler, 1896), II, 971 ff., for information on the lives and an evaluation of their validity.

2. He was a native Athenian, a member of the Cydathenaeum deme and the tribe of Pandion. His father's name was Phillipus, and either he or his father may have been a cleruch on Aegina. Three sons survived him, Ararus, Phillipus, and a third whose name is uncertain. The first was probably a dramatist. See Pauly-Wissova cited above. For a history of the period, see N. G. L. Hammond, *A History of Greece to 322 B.C.,* 2nd. ed. (Oxford: Clarendon Press, 1967).

3. Thucydides, *The Peloponnesian War,* trans. Richard Crawley, introd. John H. Finley, Jr. (New York: Modern Library, 1951), Bk II, Chs. xxxvii - xxxix (p. 104).

4. He may have been accused of lese majesty in 426. In the lost play, *Babylonians,* he criticized Cleon's harsh treatment of the allies. The hero of the *Acharnians* (425) laments that Cleon took him to court for last year's comedy (l. 377). If the trial is a fact, it must have had no serious consequences; two years later, Aristophanes attacked Cleon even more harshly in *Knights.*

5. Plutarch, *Moralia. Book I. The Education of Children,* trans. Frank Cole Babbitt (London & New York: G. P. Putnam's Sons, 1927), 10 C - D (p. 49).

6. For a detailed account, see Sir Arthur Pickard-Cambridge, *The Dramatic Festivals of Athens,* 2nd ed. rev. by John Gould and D. M. Lewis (Oxford: Clarendon Press, 1968).

7. E. R. Dodds, *Euripides' Bacchae* (Oxford: Clarendon Press, 1944), pp. ix - xviii, contains an excellent discussion of the character and worship of Dionysus.

8. Cedric H. Whitman, *Aristophanes and the Comic Hero* (Cambridge, Mass.: Harvard University Press, 1964); K. J. Dover, *Aristophanic Comedy* (Berkeley: University of California Press, 1972); and Hermann Weber, "Aristophanes and his Sense of the Comic: A Comparative Study of the Meaning of Old Comedy" (Ph.D. Diss., University of Texas, 1968), analyze the comedies from the standpoint of freedom and self-assertion.

9. For a presentation of the various theories, see Margaret Bieber,

History of the Greek and Roman Theater (Princeton: Princeton University Press, 1939); Arthur W. Pickard-Cambridge, *Dithyramb, Tragedy, and Comedy*, 2nd ed. rev. by T. B. L. Webster (Oxford: Clarendon Press, 1962); and T. B. L. Webster, *Greek Theatre Production* (London: Methuen, 1956).

10. Aristotle discusses the origin of comedy in *Poetics*, Ch. V (1449 b).

11. For a concise introduction to Greek meter, see James W. Halporn, Martin Ostwald, & Thomas G. Rosenmeyer, *The Meters of Greek and Latin Poetry* (Indianapolis: Bobbs-Merrill, 1963).

12. Gregory M. Sifakis, *Parabasis and Animal Choruses* (London: Athlone Press, 1971), argues that the parabasis was a conscious digression created by fifth-century poets.

13. T. Gelzer, *Der epirrhematische Agon bei Aristophanes*, Zetemata, No. 23 (Munich: Beck, 1960); Timothy Long, "Persuasion and the Aristophanic Agon," *Transactions and Proceedings of the American Philological Association* 103 (1972), 285 - 99; C. T. Murphy, "Aristophanes and the Art of Rhetoric," *Harvard Studies in Classical Philology* 49 (1938), 69 - 113; and Sifakis, p. 120, n. 26.

14. Sifakis, pp. 86 - 108.

15. See F. M. Cornford, *The Origin of Attic Comedy* (London: E. Arnold, 1914), for a full exposition of the ritual theory. Sifakis (pp. 15 - 20 and 110 - 13) summarizes the various explanations and includes an annotated bibliography.

16. See Peter Arnott, *Greek Scenic Conventions in the Fifth Century B.C.* (Oxford: Clarendon Press, 1962) as well as the works cited in note 9. Dover discusses problems of production of the individual comedies. See also C. W. Dearden, *The Stage of Aristophanes*, (London: Athlone Press, 1976), a study published too late for use in this book.

17. Pp. 86, 102.

18. Lillian B. Lawler, *The Dance in Ancient Greece* (Middletown: Wesleyan University Press, 1965), pp. 87 - 88.

19. The limitation on the number of actors may have developed because the chorus was the most important component at first and actors were added only gradually. Or it may be related to the expense of the production. The frequent failure to indicate change of speaker in the mss. makes assigning lines and counting actors difficult. See Dover (pp. 6 - 10) for a general explanation and J. C. B. Lowe, "The Manuscript Evidence for Change of Speaker in Aristophanes," *Bulletin of the Institute of Classical Studies of the University of London* 9 (1962), 27 - 42, and editions of individual plays for more information.

20. P. Walcot, "Aristophanic and Other Audiences," *Greece and Rome* 18 (1971), 35 - 50.

Chapter Two

1. For a detailed study of parody in Aristophanes, see Peter Rau,

Paratragodia: Untersuchung einer komischen Form des Aristophanes, Zetemata, No. 45 (Munich: Beck, 1967). He discusses *Telephus* on pp. 19 - 41.

2. Douglass Parker, trans., *The Acharnians*, The Mentor Greek Comedy (New York: New American Library, 1961), p. 118.

3. Lois Spatz, "Strophic Construction in Aristophanic Lyric" (Ph.D. Diss., Indiana University, 1968), pp. 20 - 55.

4. Weber discusses this function of comedy. See especially chapter 2, "The Tragic and Comic and the Problems of Civilization: An Interpretation of the *Peace* and the *Birds.*"

5. Pp. 59 - 65.

6. See Whitman's chapter on the *Acharnians* and especially pp. 76 - 80 for a discussion of the way the structure demonstrates Dicaeopolis' growing heroism.

7. See Weber, chapter 3, "The Obscene Comic: A Look at *Acharnians* and *Peace.*" I was unable to obtain Jeffrey Henderson's *The Maculate Muse: Obscene Language in Attic Comedy* (New Haven: Yale University Press, 1976) but judge from the review by Oliver Taplin, *Times Literary Supplement* 30 Jan. 1976, p. 107, that the book treats the use of sex in a similar way.

8. P. 38.

9. Victor Coulon, ed., and Hilaire Van Daele, trans., *Aristophane: Tome II, Les Guepes, La Paix,* 5th ed. (Paris: Budé, 1964), pp. 88 - 89.

10. Whitman, pp. 104, 310, n. 1.

11. Rau, pp. 89 - 97.

12. P. 138.

Chapter Three

1. See the edition of *Clouds* with introduction and commentary by K. J. Dover (Oxford: Clarendon Press, 1968), pp. lxxx - xcviii, for an evaluation of the evidence.

2. Whitman, pp. 123 - 37 and 314, n. 40.

3. For a detailed study of early Greek philosphy, see Kathleen Freeman, *The Pre-Socratic Philosophers: A Companion to Diels, "Fragmente der Vorsokratiker"* (Cambridge, Massachusetts: Harvard University Press, 1946). E. A. Havelock, *The Liberal Temper in Greek Politics* (New Haven, Conn.: Yale University Press, 1957) and Charles P. Segal, "Reason, Emotion, and Society in the Sophists and Democritus" (Ph.D. Diss., Harvard University, 1965) present accounts of the Sophists, their aims, and their impact on society.

4. See the fragments of Gorgias collected in Freeman, pp. 353 - 57. For a detailed study of the development of Greek prose and its relation to philosophy, see W. R. M. Lamb, *Clio Enthroned* (Cambridge: Cambridge University Press, 1914) and J. D. Denniston, *Greek Prose Style* (Oxford: Clarendon Press, 1952).

5. Euripides, *Hippolytus*, trans. David Grene in *Complete Greek Tragedies. Volume V* (New York: Modern Library, n.d.), ll. 486 - 489 (p. 200).

6. Thomas Gelzer, "Aristophanes und sein Sokrates," *Museum Helveticum* 13 (1956), 68 - 69, discusses the relation to Diogenes. William Arrowsmith, trans., *Clouds*, The Mentor Greek Comedy (New York: New American Library, 1962), pp. 136 - 37, explains and expands upon the metaphor of the cosmic oven, although he does not connect the terms specifically with Diogenes.

7. Plutarch, *Moralia. Book I. The Education of Children*, 10 C - D.

8. Edward Frankel, *Beobachtungen zu Aristophanes* (Rome: Edizioni di Storia e Litteratura, 1962), pp. 196 - 98.

9. Arrowsmith, p. 143.

10. Arrowsmith (pp. 144 - 45) accepts the scholiast who says the two discourses were dressed like fighting cocks and were brought out in cages. Dover, *Clouds*, pp. xc - xciii, however, believes that the scholiast refers to the original version of *Clouds*, not the revision that we have.

11. Murphy, pp. 69 - 98, 104; Long, pp. 294 - 95.

12. See Weber, especially chapter 5, "The Comic and the Fallacy of Reason and Rationality: *The Knights, The Clouds*, and *The Frogs*."

13. Whitman, pp. 136 - 37.

14. See Spatz, pp. 76 - 104 and also "Metrical Motifs in Aristophanes' *Clouds*," *Quaderni Urbinati* 13 (1972), 62 - 82 for a discussion of the way the rhythms underline the dramatic movement.

15. P. 124. He presents an analysis of the antinomies.

Chapter Four

1. The Court of the Areopagus had jurisdiction in cases of homicide and impiety. For information on the Athenian jury system, see Robert J. Bonner and Gertrude Smith, *The Administration of Justice from Homer to Aristotle* (Chicago: University of Chicago Press, 1930), I, 221 - 50 and J. Walter Jones, *The Law and Legal Theory of the Greeks* (Oxford: Clarendon Press, 1956), pp. 116 - 51. The former explains the way courts were organized and the latter concentrates on attitudes toward the law and the means of reaching decisions.

2. Douglas M. MacDowell, *Wasps: edited with Introduction and Commentary* (Oxford: Clarendon Press, 1971), pp. 3 - 4.

3. MacDowell, pp. 1 - 2.

4. MacDowell (pp. 249 - 61) analyzes the way in which the mock trial satirizes court procedure, forensic oratory, and typical attitudes of defendants, plaintiffs, and jurymen.

5. This parabasis is shorter than normal. Either the text is corrupt or Aristophanes has omitted some of the parts. See MacDowell's commentary on lines 1265 - 91.

6. Some editors judge that this ode is inconsistent with the raucous end-

ing and must have been misplaced. See MacDowell's commentary on lines 1450 - 71.

7. MacDowell (pp. 5 - 6) summarizes the criticism and demonstrates the unity of the play's structure. See also Whitman (pp. 156 - 61) on the importance as well as the coherence of the second part of the play.

Chapter Five

1. Whitman (p. 80) accounts for the confusion by assuming that censorship laws were difficult to enforce and summarizes the scholarship (pp. 307 - 8). Weber judges from the insufficiency of the evidence that Aristophanes may have created the idea of charges to intensify the ridicule of Cleon (pp. 53 - 54).

2. For a detailed analysis of Aristophanes' use of metaphor, see Hans Joachim Newiger, *Metapher und Allegorie: Studien zu Aristophanes*, Zetemata, No. 16 (Munich: Beck, 1957).

3. Perhaps the slaves wore masks which identified them as the two generals. Dover, however (pp. 28 - 29, 95), thinks the comic mask, with its large openings for eyes and mouth, was not conducive to recognizable portraiture. He suggests that the reference to the maskmakers' fears of Cleon (230 - 33) may have given the playwright a chance to explain his use of a hideous, if unrecognizable, mask for the demagogue.

4. Manfred Landfester, *Der Ritter des Aristophanes: Beobachtungen zur dramatischen Handlung und zum komischen Stil des Aristophanes* (Amsterdam: Gruner, 1967), develops Newiger's theories and traces this upside-down allegory as well as the lover allegory developed later.

5. Victor Ehrenberg, *The People of Aristophanes: A Sociology of Old Comedy* (New York: Schocken, 1962), discusses the economic class and behavior implicit in the occupations of the characters. See pp. 115, 120 - 21 for specific references to Cleon.

6. Bernard Knox, "The Date of the *Oedipus Tyrannus* of Sophocles," *American Journal of Philology* 77 (1956), 133 - 47.

7. Dover, p. 96.

8. See W. W. Merry, *The Birds with Introduction and Notes*, 3rd ed. (Oxford: Clarendon Press, 1896), pp. 13 - 19, for a presentation and analysis of the various theories.

9. Pp. 145 - 46.

10. Whitman, p. 167.

11. William Arrowsmith, trans., *The Birds*, The Mentor Greek Comedy (New York: New American Library, 1961), p. 11, suggests that the birds are Athens' subjects who were once her allies.

12. P. 9.

13. Dover, p. 145.

14. P. 11.

15. Pp. 176 - 77. See chapter 3 for the importance of the *nomos-physis* antithesis in the last quarter of the fifth century in Athens.

16. Whitman (pp. 172 - 76) develops this point and suggests that Aristophanes may be using the terms and ideas of Gorgias whose works seem to concern the relation between reality and language.

17. Perhaps Aristophanes has written himself into these scenes to mock his own pretensions.

18. Weber, Preface and pp. 80 - 91.

Chapter Six

1. For a full study of the subject, see Sarah B. Pomeroy, *Goddesses, Whores, Wives, and Slaves: Women in Classical Antiquity* (New York: Schocken, 1975).

2. Thucydides, *The Peloponnesian War*, trans. Richard Crawley, introd. John H. Finley, Jr. (New York: Modern Library, 1951), Bk. II, Ch. xlvi (p. 109).

3. Dover, p. 159.

4. P. 148.

5. Dover, p. 39.

6. Weber, Appendix, esp. pp. 211 - 14.

7. Although in 411 the priestess of Athena Nike was named Myrrhine and the priestess of Athena Polias was named Lysimache, Dover (p. 152) argues against theories that Aristophanes' characters are allusions to these priestesses. In fact, Aristophanes' characters' names refer to their functions. "Lysistrata" means "Dissolver of Battles," "Myrrhine" or "Perfumed" suggests the aphrodisiac she is, and "Cinesias" refers to motion and, in an obscene sense, to intercourse.

8. Victor Coulon, ed., and H. Van Daele, trans., *Aristophane: Tome III, Les Oiseaux, Lysistrata*, 5th ed. (Paris, 1958), pp. 131 - 32, n. 6. Coulon explains that here as elsewhere the chorus represents the city as a whole instead of individuals.

9. It is not clear whether they sing all the strophes together or divide up again into males and females for their remaining ode. The problem is not pressing, however, since they sing now to the audience instead of each other. See Douglass Parker, trans., *Lysistrata*, The Mentor Greek Comedy (New York, 1964), p. 122, for a possible explanation.

10. See G. W. Elderkin, "Aphrodite and Athena in the *Lysistrata* of Aristophanes," *Classical Philology* 35 (1940), 387 - 98, for a study of the references to the cults of the goddesses.

11. Whitman (pp. 205 - 14) discusses the image patterns in the play.

Chapter Seven

1. There is no external evidence for the date of performance. See Victor Coulon, ed., and H. Van Daele, trans., *Aristophane: Tome IV, Les Thesmophories, Les Grenouilles* (Paris, 1954), p. 10. Van Daele discusses why 411 B.C. is the probable date. Dover (p. 169) conjectures that it was produced at the Great Dionysia.

2. See Thucydides, *The Peloponnesian War*, Bk. VIII, Ch. lxvi.

3. The old man is never named in the manuscripts. Instead he is called *Kēdestēs* ("relative-by-marriage"). Dover (p. 165) suggests that he acts more like a poor relation than a father-in-law. Dover calls him Old Man instead of Mnesilochus, the name given him by a late Roman commentator.

4. For bibliography, see Albin Lesky, *Die tragische Dichtung der Hellenen*, 3rd ed. (Göttingen: Vandenhoeck and Ruprecht, 1972), pp. 15 - 16, 518.

5. Rau, pp. 5, 178.

6. Spatz, Diss., pp. 311 - 15.

7. Dover (pp. 188 - 89) points out that tragedies belonged to the entire community and "could be used as material for humour in the same way as agriculture and sex and war could be used."

8. See Rau (pp. 42 - 53) for a detailed analysis of the use of the *Telephus* and *Palamedes* parodies.

9. Spatz, pp. 315 - 20.

10. Rau, pp. 53 - 65.

11. Arnott, p. 62.

12. Rau, pp. 65 - 89. See Spatz (pp. 335 - 43) for a discussion of the metrical parody.

Chapter Eight

1. Victor Coulon ed., and H. Van Daele, trans., *Aristophane: Tome IV, Les Thesmophories, Les Grenouilles*, (Paris, 1954), p. 82. See Hypothesis I. Dover (pp. 180 - 83) suggests, from inconsistencies in the text, that a slightly different version may have been used for the second production.

2. Cf. *Demoi* by Eupolis, produced in 412.

3. See M. Tierney, "The Parodos in Aristophanes' *Frogs*," in *Twentieth Century Interpretations of the Frogs*, ed. David J. Littlefield (Englewood Cliffs, New Jersey: Prentice-Hall, 1968), pp. 35 - 38, for the argument that the Initiates are Orphics who worship the chthonic Dionysus and have no relation to the Eleusinian Mysteries.

4. For this interpretation, I am indebted to Charles Paul Segal, "The Character of Dionysus and the Unity of the Frogs," revised and reprinted in Littlefield, pp. 45 - 57, from its original presentation in *Harvard Studies in Classical Philology* 65 (1961), 207 - 30, and to Whitman's chapter on *Frogs*, "Death and Life."

5. Whitman, pp. 235, 325, n. 18.

6. It is unclear whether the Frog Chorus appeared on stage or whether the entire rowing scene took place outside the playing area and was only heard from a distance. Dover argues (p. 180) that the frogs were visible in colorful costume and that Dionysus rowed on some sort of machine, perhaps similar to the ekkyklema, which represented the moving boat.

7. Spatz, Diss., pp. 378 - 86.

8. Pp. 235 - 44.

9. For details of the analogy, see the edition of W. B. Stanford, *Frogs:*

Edited with Introduction, Revised Text, Commentary, and Index (London: Macmillan, 1963), p. 134.

10. Spatz, pp. 391 - 92.

11. Aeschylus was born in Eleusis around 525 B.C. He may have been charged with impiety for divulging the mysteries and then acquitted.

12. P. 184.

13. Stanford (pp. xxxv - xxxvi) summarizes Aristophanes' use of parody in general and provides a bibliography. See Rau (pp. 122 - 37) for a detailed analysis of the parodies.

Chapter Nine

1. See R. G. Ussher, *Aristophanes' Ecclesiazousae, Edited with Introduction and Commentary* (Oxford: Clarendon Press, 1973), pp. xx - xxv, for an analysis of the evidence for the date of production. This edition has been extremely helpful to the analysis presented in this chapter. Dover (p. 191) and Van Daele, in Victor Coulon, ed., and H. Van Daele, trans., *Aristophane: Tome V, L'Assemblée des Femmes, Ploutos,* 3rd ed. (Paris, 1963), p. 5, also discuss the problem of dating.

2. Douglass Parker, trans., *The Congresswomen* (Ann Arbor, 1967), p. 96.

3. P. 200.

4. P. 87.

5. Ussher, pp. xxvii - xxviii; Dover, pp. 194 - 95. K. J. Maidment, "The Later Comic Chorus," *Classical Quarterly* 29 (1935), 1 - 24, discusses the reasons for the decline in the use of the chorus.

6. Ussher, p. 232.

7. Ussher and Douglass Parker, trans., *The Congresswomen,* both cite W. H. Hess, "Studies in the *Ecclesiazousae* of Aristophanes" (Ph.D. Diss., Princeton University, 1963), pp. 17 ff. Parker uses Hess' interpretation of Agyrrhius as the focal point of the satire, whereas Ussher believes that Hess has exaggerated Agyrrhius' importance. Both agree, however, that Agyrrhius' effeminacy probably influenced Aristophanes' choice of the theme of gynocracy.

8. Ussher (p. 132) discusses whether Euvaeon alludes to an historical general, as Hess (p. 57) argues.

9. See Ussher, pp. xv - xx, for a survey of current theories and a bibliography. The most likely common source is thought to be Protagorus' *Antilogica.*

10. This character is unnamed in the manuscripts, but according to Ussher (p. 181), is probably the husband of Woman B in the prologue and the neighbor who watches Blepyrus relieve himself. Parker (p. 89) divides the earlier lines assigned to him according to Hess' interpretation. E. Frankel believes that the stingy man represents the majority view and that Chremes is made to look silly here, although he gets what he wants in the last scene. See "Dramaturgical Problems in the *Ecclesiazousae,*" in *Greek*

Poetry and Life: Essays Presented to Gilbert Murray (Oxford: Clarendon Press, 1936), p. 272.

11. C. M. Bowra, "A Love Duet," *American Journal of Philology* 79 (1958), 376 - 91. See Spatz (pp. 431 - 41) for problems of line division and meter. Frankel (p. 265) suggests that the old woman appeared on the roof of the skene.

12. I am following most editors, but Frankel (pp. 272 - 73) argues that the man is Chremes, who is late because, unlike everyone else, he has turned in his property before going to dinner.

13. See E. W. Handley, "*Chorou* in the *Plutus*," *Classical Quarterly*, n.s. 3 (1953), 55 - 61, for a summary of the textual evidence.

14. Maidment, pp. 5 - 8.

15. Spatz, pp. 444 - 46.

16. P. 207.

17. Rau, pp. 160 - 61.

18. Coulon (p. 121) suggests that in ll. 665 ff. there is a further allusion to Sophocles' *Oedipus Rex*, ll. 388 ff., when Oedipus accuses the blind priest Tiresias of seeing clearly where his profit lies.

Chapter Ten

1. For a survey and bibliography of Middle and New Comedy, see Albin Lesky, *A History of Greek Literature*, trans. James Willis and Cornelius de Heer (London: Methuen, 1966), pp. 418, 633 - 36, and 642 - 64. On Menander, see W. G. Arnott, "Young Lovers and Confidence Tricksters: The Rebirth of Menander," *University of Leeds Review* 13 (1970), 1 - 18.

2. He is responsible for the first critical edition of Aristophanes' comedies as well as a treatise on Menander and one on the character types of Greek comedy.

3. Howard North Fowler, trans., *Plutarch's Moralia*, The Loeb Classical Library (Cambridge, Massachusetts: Harvard University Press, 1936), X, 463 - 69. This translation comes from a summary of one of Plutarch's lost essays.

4. See Lesky (pp. 449 - 52) for a summary of the manuscript tradition and the scholarship.

Selected Bibliography

PRIMARY SOURCES

1. Editions of the Greek Text

Coulon, Victor, ed., and Van Daele, Hilaire, trans., *Aristophane*. 5 vols. Paris: Budé, 1954 - 1964. The best complete edition of the text with an apparatus, a French translation, and citations from other authors and the scholia.

Edmonds, John Maxwell, *The Fragments of Attic Comedy: Vol. I. Old Comedy*. Leiden: E. J. Brill, 1957. An edition with the contexts, notes, and English translations, which includes fragments from Aristophanes' contemporaries as well as from his missing plays.

The following English editions contain introductions and line-by-line commentaries on allusions and literary devices as well as on problems of text and translations.

Dover, K. J. *Clouds: Edited with Introduction and Commentary*. Oxford: Clarendon Press, 1968.

MacDowell, Douglas M. *Wasps: Edited with Introduction and Commentary*. Oxford: Clarendon Press, 1971.

Merry, W. W. *Birds: with Introduction and Notes*. Oxford: Clarendon Press, 1896.

Platnauer, M. *Peace: Edited with Introduction and Commentary*. Oxford: Clarendon Press, 1964.

Stanford, W. B. *The Frogs: Edited with Introduction, Revised Text, Commentary and Index*. 2nd ed. London: Macmillan, 1963.

Ussher, R. G. *Ecclesiazousae: Edited with Introduction and Commentary*. Oxford: Clarendon Press, 1973.

2. English Translations.

The following translations are particularly valuable because they capture the bawdiness and wit of Aristophanes and contain excellent introductions and notes on style, interpretation, and production.

Arrowsmith, William. *The Birds*. The Mentor Greek Comedy. New York: New American Library, 1961.

―――. *The Clouds*. The Mentor Greek Comedy. New York: New American Library, 1962.

Fitts, Dudley. *Four Comedies: Lysistrata, The Frogs, The Birds, Ladies' Day*. New York: Harcourt, Brace & World, 1954.

Lattimore, Richmond. *The Frogs*. The Mentor Greek Comedy. New York: New American Library, 1962.

Parker, Douglass. *The Acharnians*. The Mentor Greek Comedy. New York: New American Library, 1961.

————. *The Congresswomen*. Ann Arbor: University of Michigan Press, 1967.

————. *Lysistrata*. The Mentor Greek Comedy. New York: New American Library, 1964.

————. *The Wasps*. The Mentor Greek Comedy. New York: New American Library, 1962.

SECONDARY SOURCES

Please refer to chapter notes for works on individual plays.

ARNOTT, PETER D. *Greek Scenic Conventions in the Fifth Century B.C.* Oxford: Clarendon Press, 1962. A discussion of the stage, furnishings, and machinery, with specific reference to actual productions of extant plays.

BIEBER, MARGARET. *The History of the Greek and Roman Theater*. Princeton: Princeton University Press, 1939. A discussion of the origins and development of ancient theaters and the aspects of production.

CORNFORD, FRANCIS MACDONALD. *The Origins of Attic Comedy*. London: E. Arnold, 1914. A presentation of the ritual theory with an analysis relating comic structure to origin.

CROISET, MAURICE. *Aristophanes and the Political Parties at Athens*. Trans. J. Loeb. London: Macmillan, 1909. Aristophanes as a spokesman for the conservative, oligarchic faction.

DEARDEN, C. W., *The Stage of Aristophanes*. London: Athlone Press, 1976. A study of all facets of the production of Aristophanes' comedies.

DOVER, K. J. *Aristophanic Comedy*. Berkeley: University of California Press, 1972. A study of the humor and form of Old Comedy, followed by an analysis of the individual plays in their cultural context.

EHRENBERG, VICTOR. *The People of Aristophanes: A Sociology of Old Comedy*. New York: Schocken, 1962. A study of the real life of the people of Athens, based on information provided by Old Comedy.

GELZER, T. *Der epirrhematische Agon bei Aristophanes*. Zetemata, No. 23. Munich: Beck, 1960. An analysis of the agon according to its metrical divisions, formal structure, and dramatic function.

GOMME, A. W. "Aristophanes and Politics." *Classical Review* 53 (1938), 97 - 109. A presentation of the theory that Aristophanes cannot be identified with a specific political party or a consistent moral or didactic purpose.

HENDERSON, JEFFREY. *The Maculate Muse: Obscene Language in Attic Comedy*. New Haven: Yale University Press, 1975. A study of the nature and functions, literary and cultural, of obscenity in Old Comedy.

LAWLER, LILLIAN B. *The Dance in Ancient Greece*. Middletown: Wesleyan University Press, 1965. A study of dance steps, based on the examination of ancient terminology and pictures.

LEVER, KATHERINE. *The Art of Greek Comedy.* London: Methuen, 1956. A general introduction, with emphasis on Old Comedy, but including chapters on Archaic, Middle, and New Comedy as well, and with special attention to the cultural background.

LONG, TIMOTHY. "Persuasion and the Aristophanic Agon." *Translations and Proceedings of the American Philological Association* 103 (1972), 285 - 99. An analysis which demonstrates the epideictic rather than persuasive function of the agon.

LOWE, J. C. B. "The Manuscript Evidence for Changes of Speaker in Aristophanes." *Bulletin of the Institute of Classical Studies of the University of London* 9 (1962), 27 - 42.

MAIDMENT, K. J. "The Later Comic Chorus." *Classical Quarterly* 29 (1935) 1 - 24. An analysis which maintains that the chorus lost its central position through natural evolution rather than through economic or official pressure.

McEVILLEY, T. "Development in the Lyrics of Aristophanes." *American Journal of Philology* 91 (1970), 257 - 76. A study of Aristophanes' change from a traditional lyricist to a follower of the musical innovations of the late fifth century.

MURPHY, C. T. "Aristophanes and the Art of Rhetoric." *Harvard Studies in Classical Philology* 49 (1938), 69 - 113. The influence of rhetoric on the language, thought, and organization of the agons.

MURRAY, GILBERT. *Aristophanes: A Study.* Oxford: Oxford University Press, 1933. A general study of the complete works with special attention to the structure and development of Aristophanes' art.

NEWIGER, HANS-JOACHIM, Ed. *Aristophanes und die Alte Comodie.* Darmstadt: Wissenshaftliche Buchgesellshaft, 1975. A collection of essays by the major scholars of the genre, covering questions of form, language, production, and significance, with attention to specific passages as well as to general theories.

_____. *Metapher und Allegorie: Studien zu Aristophanes.* Zetemata, No. 16. Munich: Beck, 1957. A study of Aristophanes' use of personification, with specific analyses of Demos' household in the *Knights,* the two discourses in the *Clouds,* and *Wealth.*

NORWOOD, GILBERT. *Greek Comedy.* London: Methuen, 1931. Comedy from its beginnings to Menander, with the first half devoted to Aristophanes' predecessors and contemporaries.

PICKARD-CAMBRIDGE, ARTHUR W. *Dithyramb, Tragedy, and Comedy.* 2nd ed. revised by T. B. L. Webster. Oxford: Clarendon Press, 1962. The section on comedy discusses the evidence for its origin in the comos and Dorian scenes, as well as its unique formal elements.

_____. *Dramatic Festivals of Athens.* 2nd ed. revised by John Gould and D. M. Lewis. Oxford: Clarendon Press, 1968. A study of all aspects of the festivals and the dramatic productions.

POMEROY, SARAH B. *Goddesses, Whores, Wives, and Slaves: Women in Classical Antiquity.* New York: Schocken, 1975. A study of the real lives of women, based on archaeological and legal sources.

Pucci, Piero. "Aristofane ed Euripide: ricerche metriche e stilistiche." *Memorie della R. Accademia Nazionale dei Lincei*, ser. 8, vol. 10, 5 (1961), pp. 227 - 421. An analysis of Aristophanes' parodies of Euripidean meter, diction, and dramatic devices.

Rau, Peter. *Paratragodia: Untersuchung einer komischen Form des Aristophanes*. Zetemata, No. 45. Munich: Beck, 1967. A study of Aristophanes' parodies, with detailed comparisons with originals.

Russo, Carlo. *Aristofane, autore di teatro*. Florence: Sansorri, 1962. The theory that there are differences in tone, atmosphere, and production between plays written for the Dionysia and plays written for the Lenaea.

Sifakis, G. M. *Parabasis and Animal Choruses: A Contribution to the History of Attic Comedy*. London: Athlone Press, 1971. A presentation of the theory that the parabasis was a conscious digression invented by fifth-century poets. Contains much valuable interpretation of form and production.

Spatz, Lois. "Strophic Structure in Aristophanic Lyric." Ph.D. Diss., Indiana University, 1968. A study of inner responsion of the lyric strophes, with play-by-play analyses that trace the relation of the lyrical development to the dramatic movement of each play.

Taillardat, Jean. *Les Images d'Aristophane: Études des Langue et de Style*. 2nd ed. Paris: Societé d'Édition Les Belles Lettres, 1965. A catalogue of all the important metaphors and similes used by Aristophanes, arranged according to subject, with discussions of originality and tone.

Walcot, P. "Aristophanic and Other Audiences." *Greece and Rome* 18 (1971), 35 - 50. Demonstrates that the comedies were designed for a popular, not an elite, audience.

Weber, Hermann. "Aristophanes and his Sense of the Comic: A Comparative Study of the Meaning of Old Comedy." Ph.D. Diss., University of Texas at Austin, 1968. A definition of the comic, its devices, and its functions for the audience.

Webster, T. B. L. *Greek Theater Production*. London: Methuen, 1956. A discussion of the use of costumes, masks, and scenery from the beginning to the late Hellenistic period, with attention to production outside Athens.

————. *The Greek Chorus*. London: Methuen, 1970. The history of the choral dance, based on evidence from lyric meter, vase paintings, and reliefs.

White, John Williams. *The Verse of Greek Comedy*. London: Macmillan, 1912. A study of the structure and lyrics of all the comedies, with attention to the subdivisions of the strophes.

Whitman, Cedric H. *Aristophanes and the Comic Hero*. Cambridge, Mass.: Harvard University Press, 1964. A study of themes and literary devices, with emphasis on the special nature of comic heroism.

Index

(Theatrical and poetic terms are cited only once. Reference is made only to the page where a term is defined.)

165